NOW I
SEE YOU

NOW
OW
I SEE
YOU A

MEMOIR

NICOLE C. KEAR

ST. MARTIN'S PRESS ❧ NEW YORK

www.stmartins.com

Designed by Anna Gorovoy

Library of Congress Cataloging-in-Publication Data

Kear, Nicole C.
    Now I see you / Nicole C. Kear.—First edition.
        p. cm.
    ISBN 978-1-250-02656-9 (hardcover)
    ISBN 978-1-250-02657-6 (e-book)
    1. Kear, Nicole C.   2. Retinitis pigmentosa—Patients—United States—
Biography.   I. Title.
  RE661.R45K43 2014
  617.7'35—dc23

                                                              2014008151

St. Martin's Press books may be purchased for educational,
business, or promotional use. For information on bulk purchases, please contact
Macmillan Corporate and Premium Sales Department at 1-800-221-7945,
extension 5442, or write specialmarkets@macmillan.com.

First Edition: June 2014

10   9   8   7   6   5   4   3   2   1

For my Heart,
my Star,
and my Sun

and for David, whose love lights every darkness

AUTHOR'S NOTE

In order to protect the innocent, and the guilty, the names and identifying characteristics of people described in this book have been changed. In order to prevent this book from being a thousand pages and mind-numbingly boring, certain events have been reordered, combined, and condensed.

While I occasionally consulted journals, letters, and people who were there, for the most part, I wrote this book relying on my recollection, a thick, polluted sludge in which memories bob. They're not pristine, these memories; time can corrode them, stain them, tint them in various hues. If others dredged up their memories of the same events, they might look different. If that is the case and you feel so inclined, I invite you to write a memoir. Just change my name and, if you don't mind, make me a redhead.

It is better to light a candle than to curse the darkness.

—Ancient Proverb

NOW I
SEE YOU

PROLOGUE

My disguise was missing something.

"Almost ready," I told Esperanza, the small, dark-haired woman standing next to me. "Just one more minute."

I'd already jammed on the black knit hat reading BROOKLYN in block letters and pulled it low over my forehead. I'd zipped up the shit-colored ankle-length coat borrowed from my grandmother and raised the hood. Now only my shoes were visible, and my face.

The sunglasses: that's what I'd forgotten.

I fished a pair out of my coat pocket—Prada knockoffs that I'd bought on the street near Astor Place—and slid them over my ears. They were big and black and glamorous, very Jackie O. But I felt more like Stevie Wonder.

"I can't see a damn thing with these on," I complained.

"So take them off," Esperanza suggested, unperturbed by my getup or my bad language or my acting like a big old baby. "You don't need them."

That was not exactly true. She was right that I didn't need them to shield my eyes from the sun, since it was an overcast afternoon in March. I didn't need them, either, to shield the world from the sight of my eyes, which were normal-looking, pretty even; a forest blend of umber and olive, speckled with yellow. I did need the sunglasses, however, desperately.

"I'm trying to go incognito," I explained, "in case I run into someone I know."

"I don't think there's much risk of that." She laughed. "We haven't passed a single person since Third Avenue."

Esperanza had met me at my apartment on a tree-lined street in Brooklyn, expecting, I guess, that we'd conduct our business right there on my block. Instead, I'd led her for fifteen minutes downhill, away from the well-maintained Park Slope brownstones where my friends lived, away from the bright playgrounds my kids frequented, into the no-man's-land by the Gowanus Canal.

Now, we stood on broken sidewalk, flanked by abandoned warehouses, inhaling the stink of refuse. Whole minutes passed without a car whizzing by. It was the kind of spot a mobster would choose to shoot you at close range.

"This is where you want to do it?" she'd asked, her eyebrows raised.

"Yeah, this is perfect," I'd replied.

Then she'd asked if I was ready, which I wasn't, not by a long shot. But I'd suited up with hat, hood, and glasses, and at her direction, I'd taken the package she'd given me earlier out of my bag, rooting through boxes of animal crackers, broken crayons, and wet wipes. It was a tight white bundle roughly the size and shape of a microphone, though it weighed less, its five tubular pieces made from ultralight aluminum and held together with a black rubber band. I clutched it tightly in my right palm, as if it might come to life at any moment and attack me.

I was still not ready. I was, however, out of stalling techniques.

I'd been putting this moment off, not just since Esperanza picked me up a half hour before, but since I was nineteen years old. My arsenal of weapons for beating back the inevitable had been extensive: there'd been the distractions—sex and drama and later, the business of having babies; there'd been the denial that it was happening; and after that had become impossible, there was the hiding it from everyone else.

But now, after twelve years, I couldn't postpone it any longer and here was Esperanza, sent over by the New York State Commission for the Blind to teach me how to use a mobility cane.

I didn't see why formal training was necessary anyway; as far as I could tell, the whole process was pretty self-explanatory. Take a long stick and swing it around in front of you. If it hits something, don't go there. If it drops into a gaping abyss, don't go there either.

"I don't need this, you know," I informed Esperanza as I fiddled with the cane's rubber band. "I do fine without it."

"I know," she assured me. "But you may find it useful at nighttime or in crowded places, when your vision is at its worst. And—"

She paused, her voice dropping into a softer register: "Many people find it helpful to be trained on the cane while they still have a bit of usable vision left."

No matter how gentle Esperanza was administering my bitter pill, it still tasted like shit. I wanted to spit the nasty medicine out, just toss the cane into the canal and make a run for it. But running is precisely what I'd been doing for more than a decade and it wasn't working anymore. My diagnosis just kept catching up with me.

For the kids, I reminded myself. Vanity, pride, and fear were formidable opponents but my sense of maternal duty was stronger.

I pulled off the rubber band and the cane unfurled itself, the equal pieces snapping into place like a magic trick. I raised the sunglasses off my eyes to take a closer look. Apart from the handle, which was black, and a length of red at the tip, the cane was pristinely white, not a speck of dirt or grime anywhere. Of course, I hadn't been able to discern speck-sized details in years, so what did I know?

I lowered my glasses down again. The cane, and the world behind it, went dark.

"Maybe it's a good thing that I can't see much with these on," I observed to Esperanza. "It makes this more authentic, right? Makes me seem more blind."

Esperanza said nothing, but she was standing close enough that I could see her press her lips together in a polite smile, which said it all.

You are *blind. You're only pretending not to be.*

PART I

TIPS FOR THE (SECRETLY) BLIND

Tip #1: On receiving bad news

Do not be duped into believing that youth, or optimism, or adorable lacey underthings will protect you from bad news. These things will only ensure that the news comes as a big, fucking surprise.

1. THE MESSENGER

This is some Park Avenue bullshit, I fumed, slamming shut my copy of *100 Years of Solitude*. I'd been sitting in the well-appointed waiting room for almost an hour before the doctor called my name, and then it was only to squeeze some dilating drops into my eyes and send me back into the waiting room while they took effect. That had been a half hour ago, at least I guessed as much. Now that my pupils were fully dilated, I couldn't make out the numbers on my watch, or the print of my book, either. Which left me nothing to do but stew.

The whole thing was a massive waste of time. There was nothing wrong with my vision apart from near-sightedness; my regular ophthalmologist, Dr. Lee, had said so before she referred me here, "just to be extra sure." It had seemed like a fine idea at the time, but that was before I'd pissed away the better part of a summer afternoon in a waiting room.

Of course, I had nowhere else to be, really. Having just returned to New York for summer break after my sophomore year in college, I had nothing lined up until my acting apprenticeship started at the Williamston Theatre Festival in a few weeks. I'd spent the last few days bumming around the city, sleeping late in my childhood bed, seeing old friends, and taking care of annoying bits of business like this doctor's visit. That, and crying uncontrollably.

Not a day had passed since I left Yale that I hadn't broken down in tears, weeping with the kind of brio only a teenager can manage. The crying was very time-consuming, and once you factored in the hours I spent rereading old journal entries and tearing up photographs, really, there weren't enough hours in the day. Of course, breaking up is hard to do, especially for the first time.

I'm gonna call him, I decided as I stared at the blurry blue book jacket on my lap. But by the time I located a pay phone, near the bathroom, my belated sense of dignity showed up and stayed my hand. Plus, I didn't have a quarter.

It's pointless anyway, I reasoned, a familiar lump forming in my throat. I'd called him yesterday and the day before that and always, the answer was the same. The romance had run its course. Frog Legs and I were through.

Frog Legs earned his name after my grandmother saw Sam in his boxers one morning when he was staying at my parents' over spring break.

"*Il Ranocchio!*" she attempted in a whisper. Nonny's whispers never really pan out; she is permanently set on town crier mode, like she's got a built-in megaphone in her vocal cords. I shot her a reprimanding look, which triggered her giggling, which blossomed into a guffaw, until that crazy Italian had to take a seat so she didn't have a heart attack from the exertion of howling with laughter.

"What'd she say?" asked Sam, smiling. Having been raised by psychologists, in a home where respectful communication reigned, it didn't even occur to him that my grandmother might be openly deriding him.

"Oh, she's just razzing me, you know, about having a boyfriend." I ran my fingers through his dark, wavy hair and glared at Nonny.

After that, the big joke in the family was that my boyfriend had lady legs. A few months after our breakup, I was able to see the humor in this, but at the beginning of the summer, when the heart-ache was still fresh, every mention of Frog Legs had me bawling like a kid whose ice cream fell off the cone. Yes, Sam was my double scoop of ice cream with sprinkles, except that he hadn't fallen off the cone; he'd jumped.

I'd met Sam in a Shakespeare scene study class required for our theater major and we'd fallen hard for each other while rehearsing the *Romeo and Juliet* balcony scene. Just like those star-crossed lovers, though, our relationship was intense but brief. After four months together, Sam broke up with me at the end of sophomore year. We'd been fighting for a few weeks but the final nail in the coffin was when I sneaked into his email account while he was in the shower. I was shocked to discover an email he'd written to a friend in which my beloved had described me as "high maintenance" and "clingy." When Sam came out of the shower, I was in tears, begging him for an explanation.

"You read my emails?" he asked, shocked. I guess that was a first for him.

"Just this once," I sputtered. "Hardly ever." I saw his face set, like a decision had been made. I started talking fast: "But that's not the point. Let's stay on the subject! Which is, I just love you so much! I mean, these have been the best four months of my life!"

"Okay, listen," he said, sitting next to me on the edge of the bed and putting his hand on my arm. "You're great—"

"No! I won't listen to this! I DO NOT ACCEPT THIS!"

"Nicole, come on, let's—"

"Please!"

"Can you just—"

"Please!"

Because, as everyone knows, men dig batty broads with no self-respect.

When it was clear he would not be caving to my charm, I collapsed on the floor and wailed, full-on blubbered—with drool, so much that I choked on it from time to time, sending me into a heightened paroxysm of agony because I realized full well that Sam seeing me choke on my drool probably ruled out getting back together.

It was a shining moment for womankind.

Back in New York for summer break, I was continuing my meltdown at a low simmer. Every little thing I saw—pumpernickel bagels, Dr. Zizmor ads on the subway—reminded me of Sam. Even the MEN'S BATHROOM sign in the doctor's office triggered a Sam flashback. He used to use public restrooms. God, how I loved him. I fought back tears as I regarded my blurry reflection in the women's room mirror.

My hair was beyond help; the heat and humidity had wilted my fine, shoulder-length locks until they hung lifelessly off my head like yarn. I fluffed up the hair on the top of my head with my fingertips but it sunk back down instantly, limp and defeated. My mascara was smudged from the inordinate amount of sweating I'd done on the short walk from Victoria's Secret and there were circles under my eyes that concealer hadn't concealed. But in between the circles and the mascara, my eyes themselves were resplendent.

The pupils had been dilated so much, the irises were eclipsed; all that remained was a thin ring of hazel around the perimeter. It was just an accent, a border separating the black of my eye from the white. The unbroken black reflected the light so that my eyes shone, as if they were a source of illumination themselves. Big and round and colorless, my eyes were nothing short of hypnotic.

I wish Sam could see me like this, I mused. *He'd totally take me back.*

I'd made it a whole ten seconds without thinking of him: a record. I commended myself as I walked back to my seat in the waiting room to resume staring at the wall.

I should have rescheduled this crap. I'm in no state, I thought. *Damn Dr. Lee and her extreme thoroughness.*

I'd been seeing Dr. Lee for years, ever since I failed the standard high school eye exam when I was thirteen. Dr. Lee was a colleague of my father's, like all the doctors I'd ever been to, and her office was around the corner from his cardiology practice in Brooklyn Heights, where my mother was office manager/physician assistant/ consigliere. The location was convenient considering how fond my mother was of crashing my doctors' appointments. She claimed that she showed up to secure me VIP treatment ("Or else you'll waste all goddamned day in the waiting room!") but I think she was experimenting with how much humiliation a teenager can withstand before requiring psychiatric intervention. I had grown accustomed to her bursting through the door of the exam room when I was at the dermatologist's, calling him by his first name and telling him to *please* explain to me that if I *just* stopped eating chocolate, I wouldn't have *any* blackheads at *all*. So it didn't even register on the embarrassment spectrum when she acted as armchair ophthalmologist during my first eye exam, offering an unending commentary as Dr. Lee wrote out a contact lens prescription.

"It's just so strange, because everyone in our family has great eyes—none of us wear glasses—although you know what? I told her that if she kept on reading in the dark it would ruin her eyes. This one, with the books! I mean, don't get me wrong, reading is good, of course, but you can take a good thing too far, for God's sake! I hate to say it, I really do, but I was right. I mean, was I right, Eleanor?"

"She's just a little near-sighted." Dr. Lee smiled. "She'll pop in contacts and be perfect again."

Every year, I'd check in with Dr. Lee to keep current with my prescription and eventually, my mom stopped crashing my visits (she had two younger daughters to mortify) and I came to actually enjoy my annual checkup. The office was inviting; a light floral scent lingered in the waiting room and it was always the perfect temperature, even on the most sweltering summer day. I genuinely liked Dr. Lee, who was young, smart, and soft-spoken with a low-key approach and a chin-length black bob that never grew any longer. I was interested in anecdotes about her two little kids and she always wanted to hear about what I was reading. The last time I'd seen her, over spring break, I'd mentioned something I'd been wondering about.

"It was so weird," I explained at the end of the visit as she updated my chart. "I went to Montauk recently and everybody else was oohing and ahhing over the stars but I couldn't see anything. It's no big deal or anything—I just thought I'd mention it because, you know, I was the only one who couldn't see them."

I didn't really care one way or the other about being able to make out the constellations, but the trip to Montauk had reminded me of another trip, when I was ten and my parents had dragged my sisters and me at 3:00 A.M. to the southernmost tip of Staten Island to see Halley's Comet. My dad had been berserk with excitement over what he kept referring to as "*literally* a once-in-a-lifetime event." He'd even shelled out two hundred dollars for a telescope, causing my mother to mutter "What are we, made of money?" nonstop for two weeks. On the night of the big event, my family stood shivering on the beach for an hour or two before my father finally shouted triumphantly that he'd found it and it looked like a fuzzy snowball. When it was my turn at the telescope, no matter how much I squinted, I couldn't see jack. Not a hint of a smudge. But I'd oohed and ahhed along with everyone else, secretly hoping the next once-in-a-lifetime event wouldn't be such a letdown.

Nine years later, it struck me as strange that I couldn't see comets, or stars either, and I asked Dr. Lee if maybe I needed stronger contacts.

"Your prescription seems pretty good," she mused, looking through my file. "And everyone's eyes adjust to the dark differently, so I'm really not concerned. But since you're here, let's just dilate your pupils and take a look."

A half hour later, she was tilting my head back and peering into my eyes with her flashlight. "Hmmm," she murmured. "Hmmm."

"What is it?" I asked. "Hmmm" is never what you want to hear in a doctor's office.

"Oh, it's nothing," she replied, turning her light off. "I mean, I see a little something but I'm ninety percent sure it's nothing. Just to be safe, I'm going to send you to Dr. Hall so he can check it out."

"Oh," I said. "Okay."

"It's nothing." She smiled. "I just think, better safe than sorry. Sound good?"

"Sounds good," I confirmed.

And it did. As a doctor's daughter, I was accustomed to following up just to make sure. So I made an appointment with Dr. Hall for the next time I'd be back in the city, in early June, and I promptly forgot all about it. Then, one morning after I returned home from summer break, as I sobbed while rereading Frog Legs's love letters, heavily sprinkled with Shakespeare quotes, I got a call from Dr. Hall's office confirming my appointment for that Monday.

I considered postponing the appointment but "I have to phone-stalk my ex" didn't seem like an adequate excuse. *Better just to get it over with*, I thought, *check it off my to-do list.*

"Yeah sure," I sniffled to the receptionist, "I'll be there."

In an attempt to pull myself back together, fake-it-til-you-make-it style, I'd gotten dressed up the morning of the visit, in a denim mini-skirt covered with blue butterflies and a diaphanous white blouse I'd stolen from my little sister's closet. I'd caught the express train and gotten to midtown in no time, which had left me with a half hour to kill. Convenient, seeing as there was a blowout start-of-summer sale at the Victoria's Secret around the corner from the doctor's office. As I hooked on half-price bras in the dressing room, I felt a rush of optimism.

My rack looks huge in this, I thought. *Screw Sam and his lady legs.*

I bought a black lace demi-cup and matching French-cut underwear and rushed over to the doctor's office, the pink shopping bag swinging on my arm, feeling almost cheerful. By the time I was finally summoned by Dr. Hall into an exam room though, my cheerfulness had entirely dispersed.

Dr. Hall was fat and sweaty and wore wire-rimmed glasses. Like Dr. Lee before him, he peered into my pupils, but he was quick about it and didn't make any Sherlock Holmes-y sounds. I took this as a good sign.

Then he pulled up a stool and put his hands together on his lap.

"I'd like to ask you a few questions," he said.

"Ummm, okay," I replied, my eyebrows furrowing, "Is everything okay?"

"Let's just get through some questions first, all right?"

First? I thought. *Before what? Before he clears me?*

I nodded, suppressing a sigh. There was such a thing as being too thorough.

"Are you accident-prone?" he began, leaning back in his stool. "Were you considered clumsy as a child, often bumping into things?"

It was such a peculiar question, I didn't know how to respond for a second. I couldn't fathom how my childhood grace, or lack thereof, had anything to do with me not being able to see the stars now. Besides, I hadn't been an especially clumsy child, had never broken a limb, never been to the ER for stitches. I'd been a regular kid. Normal.

"Umm, no, I don't think I've ever been accident-prone, really," I replied. "I mean, sometimes I bump into things, like everyone. Nothing memorable."

He nodded.

"Although," I went on, "last summer, one night I tripped over this massive tree root on the beach and it ripped up my thigh, which was crazy, because I didn't think a tree root could be so, you know, dangerous. I probably should've got stitches but I was with my friends and we just . . . anyway, it's okay now. You can hardly even see the scar."

"Uh-huh," he grunted, weighing my answer. I instantly regretted having said so much.

"Of course, that's not being accident-prone," I added quickly. "I mean, that's just being human." Instinctively, I yanked on the hem of my miniskirt, pulling it down to cover the waterfall-shaped scar on the front of my right thigh.

Dr. Hall crossed his arms in front of his chest: "Did you play ball sports as a child?"

Was this a getting-to-know-you game? How much information was I supposed to offer about my childhood interests? Would he be inquiring next about my favorite ice-cream flavors?

"I didn't really like sports," I replied. "I've always been more of a bookworm. I'm an English and theater major."

It was odd to have him fire off the questions without taking any notes. I mean, the questions were odd to begin with, but without him recording my answers, it felt like he already knew what they would be.

"Why didn't you like sports?" he pressed on. "Was it hard to excel at them?"

"I'm sorry, but I don't know what this has to do with anything." I was starting to feel exasperated.

"Just bear with me please."

Dr. Hall seemed equally exasperated. I could tell he was anxious to move it along, get this ordeal over with so he could call in the next patient and interrogate them about their T-ball batting average.

"Honestly, I don't know." I sighed, tightening the backs on the silver hoops in my earlobes. "I didn't really like sports and I wasn't that great at them, either."

"Uh-huh," he muttered cryptically, bobbing his head. "Uh-huh."

My response seemed to be exactly what Dr. Hall was looking for, and this realization made me angry. I felt like I was playing a game I'd never heard of with someone who knew the rules and had seen all my cards. This game sucked. I wanted out.

"Do you have your driver's license?" he asked.

"No," I shot back. I wasn't accustomed to being so discourteous to authority figures, doctors in particular, but I had the distinct feeling that I was under some kind of attack and it was instinct to try and protect myself.

"Why is that?"

"You don't need a car in New York City."

I was not about to tell him that my Driver's Ed instructor, Al Corbassi of Staten Island, had stopped the car after my third lesson and told me flatly that he'd return my money but he couldn't teach me to drive. My head wasn't in the game, Al explained. I couldn't change lanes without nearly bashing into the vehicle next to me, I went through dozens of stop signs, and I kept veering into the parked cars. "You'll try again another time," Al reassured me, before having me drive myself home for the last time.

Realizing he'd hit a wall with the questions, Dr. Hall rolled his stool a little closer and asked, "Can you see my hand?"

"What?" I asked, my face hot now, my voice rising. "I don't know what you're talking about."

"This hand. Can you see it?"

I turned my head to the right and there, a few feet away, was Dr. Hall's big, meaty paw waving its sausage fingers.

"Yes, I see it now!" I exclaimed. "It's right there!" I felt a sense of urgency, like I was sprinting across a subway platform to jump onto a train car just as the doors were slamming shut. And I'd made it, I thought, had gotten onto the train before it pulled out of the station. I'd seen his hand.

But it was too late. Dr. Hall turned his back to me to jot down some notes, and the length of time he spent writing made it clear that I hadn't passed his tests, any of them. If I had, there'd be precious little to write.

I've answered all his questions, I thought as I watched him scribble in my file, *but he's not clearing me. He's not saying good luck at school and have a nice day.*

It was obvious, too, that by failing the tests, I'd confirmed some hunch he had. I was furious that Dr. Hall wasn't bothering to mask his satisfaction in having his hunch—whatever the hell it was—confirmed. But more than my anger, I felt a mounting wave of terror building.

I joined my hands together on my lap and squeezed. My heart was racing.

Something is wrong, I realized. *Something has happened.*

Finally, Dr. Hall pushed the top of his pen to retract the point and leaned out the door of the exam room, calling his nurse.

"Set her up for an ERG," he instructed.

"What's that?" I asked quietly. I wasn't angry anymore. I'd be good, I'd be compliant, and maybe he'd like me enough to say I could go, that everything was fine.

"It's an electroretinogram test. It measures the electrical response of your retina to light," he said. "We can do it for you now and when it's done, I'll take a look at the results and we'll talk about it."

I followed the nurse into another exam room where she put more drops into my eyes. Then she pulled over a big, mean-looking machine with lots of red and black wires.

"I'm just going to place these electrodes onto your eyes," she explained.

I wondered if that matter-of-fact delivery ever worked for her, if people ever just said, "Cool, whatever." I raised my hand in front of me in a "halt" gesture.

"Electrodes?" I repeated.

"Yes, they're basically contact lenses with the electrodes attached," she reassured me. "Don't worry, your eyes have been anaesthetized; you won't feel a thing."

It doesn't take many trips to the doctor to learn you can't believe them when they feed you that line. The electrodes didn't hurt exactly, but they were bulky and heavy and caused me to blink involuntarily. This was unfortunate—and a serious design flaw, I decided—because every time I blinked, the electrodes would pop out. Then the nurse would sigh in a castigating way and reinsert them, first covering the lenses with goop, whose purpose, I guessed, was to help transmit the electricity from my retinas. This goop made my eyes tear incessantly, which made me blink, which started the process all over again.

I tried to pretend it was a game—a staring contest like the kind I played as a kid—but the punishing process of keeping my eyes pried open with those grotesque versions of contacts itching like mad was nothing like child's play. I fought against the muscles of my face, which conspired to squeeze my lids shut and expel the foreign objects lodged inside. I tried not to think about A *Clockwork Orange*. I tried not to think about how intensely pleasurable it would be to drop my lids shut, just for a second, relief like cool water running down your throat on a scorching day.

So, the nurse was dead wrong; I *could* feel things, all sorts of things, and none of them were pleasant.

"I need you to stop blinking." It was part order, part rebuke.

"Sorry," I replied. "I'm trying."

But I lost the stare-off, again, and out popped another contact.

"The more you blink, the longer we're here." She pointedly squirted fresh goop on the torture device and reinserted it onto the surface of my eye.

I swallowed hard to keep myself from crying. If blinking annoyed her this much, imagine how apoplectic she'd be if I broke down in tears. It occurred to me that it probably wasn't the smartest idea to apply mascara that morning. Then again, I'd expected a few drops and some flashlights, not electrodes.

Finally, the nurse had gotten what she needed and handed over a bunch of tissues to mop up the goop that was oozing out of my eyes. I let my top lids drop and relished the cool, quiet easiness of not looking. Being able to close my eyes whenever I felt like it was a terrific luxury, one I'd entirely taken for granted.

You don't know what you've got . . . , I thought.

The nurse held on to my elbow and led me back into the first exam room, because with all the drops and the goop, I could hardly see anything. I sat back in the exam chair, eyes shut as my relief was replaced with foreboding.

Everything might still be okay, I reminded myself. *There's been no bad news.* But there was a "yet" that followed the thought, and I knew that I should brace myself for impact.

I heard the door open and a rotund figure waddled in. Dr. Hall regarded the ERG printout for a minute and then he spoke, slowly, deliberately.

"Now, I want you to remember that I'm just the messenger here," he began. "Don't shoot the messenger."

"What is it?" I asked.

"You have a degenerative retinal disease." He paused, waiting for a response, but I sat there, silent, so he went on.

"It's called retinitis pigmentosa and it's genetic, even in your case, where no one in your family has it. Essentially, the photoreceptor cells in your retina, the ones that turn light into electrical impulses for the brain, are dying."

He paused.

I should not be here alone, I thought. *I wish my mother were here.*

"The disease usually begins by destroying your rods, responsible for night vision and peripheral vision, which explains you bumping into things and your trouble at nighttime. The degeneration of the cones, which are responsible for central vision, typically comes later on, though how much later depends on the individual patient."

There were tears sliding down my face, from the goop. I wasn't crying. I felt like it was important to tell the doctor this.

"I'm not crying," I said. "It's just the goop."

"I understand," he replied.

Then I asked him if he meant I was going blind.

"Now, please, remember, I'm just the messenger," he stammered. He seemed nervous, which was disconcerting.

I couldn't imagine this was standard protocol for delivering bad news. It seemed unlikely that in medical school, the professor of Intro to Bedside Manners had instructed a younger, thinner Dr. Hall to sprinkle his diagnosis with the phrase "don't shoot the messenger." Was I even sure this joker was fully licensed? I knew more about breaking unfavorable medical news than he did, and my wealth of knowledge was gleaned entirely from overhearing my father on the phone and watching prime-time hospital dramas.

"As I said, the loss of vision happens at a different rate for everyone," he continued. "Some people become legally blind, some retain light perception, others lose all vision. Some sooner than others. It's impossible to predict. So far your progression has been fairly slow, so all we can do is hope that it continues that way and that you have another ten, maybe fifteen years with lots of usable vision left."

My vision had just been given an expiration date. That seemed a bad sign.

"So the answer is yes, then," I clarified. "I am going blind."

"In a manner of speaking."

"In what manner of speaking?" I shot back. There was no point in being polite anymore. "I mean, it's not figurative, is it? I'm not losing my perspective. I'm going blind."

Dr. Hall said nothing.

"So what medicine can I take?" I ventured. "Or do I need an operation?"

"Unfortunately, at this time . . . ," he began, and hearing his tone switch from upbeat to regretful was enough of an answer to make me stop listening. There was no cure, no treatment. This was the real deal, an old-school affliction where you get it, you're fucked, case closed. But as my mind fell with increasing speed into despair, I clung for a moment to a ledge of doubt.

"How can you be sure? How can you be sure that I have this?"

Dr. Hall unfolded the ERG printout and handed it to me. Although it was blurred, the chart was easy to make out. It was more or less a straight line.

"This is supposed to be sinusoidal," he said, "with ups and—"

I cut him off: "I know what sinusoidal means."

"It's supposed to show peaks in electrical activity when your retina responds to the light," he explained. "But in your case, we're not seeing those peaks."

There's no equivocation in a graph that should be wavy but is flat. Staring at that flat line, I knew no second opinion was necessary.

"This is going to affect the way you live your life," Dr. Hall went on, "and in a way, you're in a fortunate position now because you're just starting out. You're going to want to consider this factor as you choose a career, and a place to live, and a partner."

I closed my eyes. Dr. Hall disappeared, along with his flat-line graph and the eye chart on the wall behind him. It wasn't exactly darkness I found behind my eyelids; it was just absence, nothingness. I wondered if that was what blindness would be like.

"You're going to want to start making changes," I heard Dr. Hall say. I opened my eyes and found him leaning forward, looking at me intently.

"Do you understand?" he asked.

"Yes," I replied.

But I didn't. I didn't have a fucking clue.

Tip #2: On sharing the news

There is no good way to break the news of your incurable degenerative disease to loved ones.

Not the weirdly upbeat delivery ("So, guess who's going blind?"). Not the made-for-TV-movie approach ("There's something I need to tell you; are you sitting down?"). Not the downplayed, bratty teen approach ("So my eyeballs are rotting. Whatever."). All the ways bum people out.

Prepare for tears. Gifts of talismans. Sudden and impassioned religious gestures such as the laying on of hands and benediction with holy water. None of this is likely to make you feel better. It may, in fact, freak you the hell out, and cause you to determine that this news is the kind best kept private. Just be sure you know what you're getting into. You may find yourself a grown-ass woman in a disguise holding a mobility cane. Stranger things have happened.

2. MY FATHER'S STUDY

It's an unsettling sensation to witness your past getting a major re-write. It was like Dr. Hall had run a "find and replace" search on the document of my life; for every instance of "clumsy," replace with "blind."

I kept thinking of a book I'd read when I was about eight, a slim paperback about Helen Keller's childhood. The illustration on the cover was framed in black and showed Helen, about the same age I was when I read it, blindfolded with a white cloth, holding a cat against her chest. I'd devoured the book, like I did so many, in an afternoon, and had read a chunk of it while following my mother around Cangiano's Italian supermarket. I'd been so engrossed in the book, in fact, that I'd walked into a display of discounted biscotti and caused a cookie avalanche.

"Would you pay attention to where you're going?" my mother had hissed. "Put the damn book down for a minute!"

So I did, turning my attention instead to picking out what kind of ravioli we were going to have for dinner. There was no way I could have guessed that the reason I bumped into the biscotti wasn't because I was a bookworm with her head in the clouds but because the cells in my retina were degenerating. Now, a decade later, I kept replaying this scene in my mind, thinking of a phrase I'd recently learned in an Intro to Theater Studies lecture: dramatic irony. As a privileged kid with no impediments, really, of any kind, I'd felt so sad for Helen, so sorry for her. Now the girl with the blindfold was me.

All those accidents I'd had over the years—smashing my forehead into lampposts, bashing my shins into coffee tables, face-planting when I tripped over fire hydrants—they weren't because I was an airhead who didn't pay attention. They were because I had one-third the field of vision that everyone else had; instead of a wide arc, 180 degrees, I had a narrow strip of 60 down the middle. I was a horse wearing blinders, ones that blocked out the world not just on the sides but on the top and the bottom, too, and weird little patches in between. And that was at my best, during the day, with all the lights on. In dimly lit places and at nighttime, it was as if I were wearing a dark veil, one I couldn't take off.

I wasn't a fan of this Blind Rewrite; the whole thing was maudlin, overblown. I wanted to revert to the original where I was a ditzy blonde, because in that story everything worked out okay. In the new story, where some disease was nibbling holes in my vision like a mouse gnawing through a slice of cheddar, everything did not work out okay. Suddenly, somehow, I'd been screwed out of a happy ending.

In the weeks that followed my diagnosis, I made a good show of carrying on with business as usual to boost my family's morale, but I spent most of my waking hours trying to figure out what had happened in that doctor's office. Was this new information a game changer? What did it actually mean for my future? Dr. Hall had talked about making changes in my life but I was damned if I knew what changes he meant. Was he implying I start pinning socks together in the washing machine? Learn Braille? What did blind people do, anyway? From what I'd gleaned over the past nineteen years, there were three options: penning epic poems (Homer/Milton); composing musical masterpieces (Ray Charles/Stevie Wonder); and selling pencils out of paper cups (homeless people). Slim pickings.

Incessantly, I worried that the diagnosis meant I couldn't have kids. My children were only conceived of in my mind, but they were fully formed. I had dreamt of them since I was a little girl, swaddling my Cabbage Patch dolls and imagining what I'd name my real babies one day, what songs I'd sing to them at bedtime. I'd imagined my children every night I babysat for the neighbor's kids, every summer I worked as a camp counselor, every time I cooed at an infant in an elevator. And now I couldn't, in good conscience, have them.

Could I? I'd never heard of a blind person having kids. How could I change dirty diapers or bandage scrapes if I couldn't see? How could I avoid walking the stroller into a manhole? Plus, even though I was the first in my family to have the disease, it was genetic and I could pass it on to my children. Wouldn't that be selfish? All signs on the road to motherhood seemed to say, "Proceed no further. What are you, fucking crazy?"

But childlessness was just the tip of the iceberg. How was I going to work? How would I be a star of stage and screen? Who would find me sexy when I couldn't apply eyeliner or pick out my own outfits? How in the hell would I have the fabulous life that I was on the cusp of beginning?

I forced myself to get out of the house, but no matter where I was, one insidious fear kept slipping in. It was disconcerting because, having always been a perky, optimistic girl, I wasn't used to macabre musings. I felt like the ghost of Sylvia Plath was invading my body, an experience that, for the record, sucks balls. I'd be in the communal dressing room at Joyce Leslie in the West Village, trying on swimsuits, when all of a sudden the thought would surface. It was a calm, cold report:

Right now, my eyes are dying. Today, I see less than yesterday. Tomorrow, I'll see less than today. It will keep getting darker, little by little, like night falling, until the last sliver of sun has

set and all the light has died. There is nothing I can do to stop
it. There is nothing I can do. There is nothing.

Inarguably, a downer. But not as much of a downer as the general atmosphere in my house.

My parents shuffled around like someone had turned up the gravity dial and it was a struggle to stay standing. Every time I saw my grandmother, she'd start crying and muttering her rosary in Italian, thus creating a vortex of gloom so intense it could've sucked the cheer out of Disneyland. An incurable neurotic, she'd spent my whole life worrying about my sisters and cousins and me—calling the police if we were a half hour late getting home from high school, force-feeding us chicken soup when we had the flu—and now, it had finally happened. The nasty twist of Fate she was preparing herself for had arrived and there was nothing she could do to fix it.

There'd been a period of real panic immediately after my visit to Dr. Hall when it dawned on everyone that since my disease was genetic, other members of my family could have it, too; at particular risk were my sisters, Marisa, seventeen, and Jessica, nine. It had been a tense week or so before everyone could get appointments with a retinal specialist (not Dr. Hall, never Dr. Hall again), but finally, it was determined that my sisters, parents, cousins, aunts, and uncles were all unaffected. The crisis was contained in me. Of course by that point, my parents had had ample time to contemplate what it meant, in practical terms, for their nineteen-year-old to be going blind. I can only imagine what they imagined because we didn't talk about it, but if their hunched shoulders and downturned eyes were any indication, the outlook was not rosy.

I'm sure they were trying hard to mask their grief, but hiding intense emotion has never been a skill my family members possess. It was clear that they were devastated, and this frightened me. I was trying to formulate my own reaction to the diagnosis, and their sadness did not point me in a positive direction. No, the message I was getting was pretty much: "Abandon all hope, ye who enter here."

About a week after the diagnosis, I walked into my father's study and found him crying. At first, I didn't notice he was crying. What I noticed when I walked into his home office, located off the kitchen, was the massive medical volume lying open on his desk. I'd never seen one of those behemoths off the shelf before; until then, I'd suspected they were a front, like a hollowed-out Bible that houses a flask or a pistol. But now my father was sitting at his huge oak desk, always so neatly organized, with his narrow shoulders slumped over the book. The gooseneck clip light was on and he was wearing his reading glasses, turning the tissue-paper pages.

"What are you doing?" I ventured.

He turned to me, and his face looked so crumpled and sagging, I instantly regretted saying anything.

He looks so old, I thought.

"Come here, honey," he said, beckoning me over to a wooden chair near his desk. Then he smiled, one of those sad smiles people muster up to make you feel better but that have the exact opposite effect.

"I want to tell you—," he started, and then his voice broke off and he removed his glasses.

My father is not an unemotional man—he gets visibly angry and disappointed and excited—but I'd never seen him cry before, not even when his mother or father or brother died. My dad is the fix-it guy. He repairs things. If you've got a splinter, he takes it out. If you've got an infection, he prescribes antibiotics. If you're on vacation and there are five of you and only one bed, he fashions luxuriously comfy sleeping surfaces out of suitcases and outerwear. Broken toasters, wilted orchids, malfunctioning heart valves—there is nothing my father cannot fix. Almost nothing.

I'd known the diagnosis was bad but watching my father cry, it seemed worse than bad. It seemed insurmountable.

"I just want to tell you that I'm sorry," he managed, wiping his face briskly. "It's my fault. I gave you my genes, and they did this to you."

As the Park Avenue doc had explained it, since there was no family history of the disease, mine was probably a spontaneous mutation, which meant that my father's self-flagellation was, technically, unwarranted. Which would've been helpful to mention had I not been struck dumb, as well as half blind.

"If one of the genes was just a little different, this wouldn't be happening," he went on.

"It's okay," I croaked.

"I wish I could take this off of you and put it onto me. You don't deserve this."

The lump in my throat was getting unmanageably big, and I knew any second, the only thing that could make the situation worse was about to happen, and I'd start crying, too. Pretty soon, my dad and I would be bawling in stereo, and the sound of that sobfest would attract my mother and sisters, and then everyone would be weeping like a goddamned Greek chorus. This had to end, now. I cleared my throat.

"It's not your fault, Daddy," I began with confidence. "And it is going to be all right. There is a lot of promising research and I'm young so there's plenty of time. It's going to be all right."

I made up the shit about "promising research." I mean, there probably was some mad scientist somewhere injecting stuff into rat retinas or reconstituting cadaver eyeballs, and for the purposes of this emergency pep talk, these endeavors qualified as "closing in on a cure." I must have sounded convincing because my father smiled.

He took my hand and squeezed it. Then he put a bookmark in his medical book, closed it, and told me he was going to bed.

I, on the other hand, might never sleep again. Seeing my father cry was more harrowing than having electrodes attached to my eyes. Whatever else happened, I had to make sure I never saw my father cry again on my account, because I might not make it through the next episode with my wits intact. I'd have to deliver on my pep talk, make sure it did turn out all right. The first step was clear: get the hell out of Bleak House. That was easy enough, as I had to report to my post as acting apprentice in Williamstown shortly.

But there was another, more important step I needed to take to turn things around: from now on, I'd keep my depressing disease to myself. It was becoming clear that I'd have enough on my plate without having to deal with the pity and concern of other people. Unlike leprosy or elephantiasis, nobody would know about my disease unless I told them—for now, at least. And I had a right to privacy, I reasoned; I had a right not to be reduced to The Tragic Case. As far as my family was concerned, not only did I have a right, I had a responsibility.

Tip #3: On handshakes

When you lack peripheral vision, handshakes can be a real pain in the ass. You'll inevitably leave folks hanging with their palms splayed out expectantly, and they will have no choice but to conclude you're a stone-cold bitch.

Thankfully, there's an easy solution. Be aggressively friendly and beat your partner to the shake. As soon as you sniff an introduction in the works, shoot your right hand out like a ramrod. With lousy depth perception, you may misjudge how close they're standing and end up making contact with your potential friend's solar plexus instead of their hand. Should that occur, act like it was fully intentional by rubbing the fabric of their shirt between your fingers, offering a relevant observation, for example: "What is this, cashmere? Or is it a blend?"

This tactic works best when your partner is donning linen or silk or worsted wool, and less well when they are wearing, say, a white Fruit of the Loom T-shirt soaked through with sweat from their morning jog. Still, at worst they'll assume you're a flirt (not necessarily a bad thing) or that you're an eccentric with a background in textile arts (even better).

3. CARPE DIEM

If I had hair like that, I'd be smiling, too, I thought as I slammed my hammer down. For a second, I felt better. Pounding nails into wood has that effect. Then I realized I hadn't driven the nail in, only flattened it on top of the wood like roadkill.

"Sonofabitch," I muttered. It was my grandmother's favorite curse and always made her feel better. But my mood was too far gone. Not even a fancy expletive like "holy mother of shitballs" could do the trick.

It was clear: I had no future in construction. Which was fine by me. I didn't want to be building the sets for the Williamstown Theatre Festival in the first place; I wanted to be treading on them, as an actor. I didn't want to be hanging lights or Xeroxing scripts, either, but none of that was as bad as building sets because not only was I piss-poor at it, but a construction site is no place for a half-blind person. Navigating my way across the set-in-progress, I felt like a character in a video game, trying to step over nails, saws, and screw guns, trying to dodge lumber as it was carried around—all with tunnel vision.

I'd imagined that my gig as acting apprentice would involve more Molière master classes, less coffee runs. I was, consequently, pretty disgruntled. Ruby though, a fellow apprentice, didn't seem to mind in the least. I knew this because my eyes had been glued to her, with a pathetic envy, for the past few days.

Ruby was no traffic-stopping beauty, but she had stupefying auburn hair—the kind of ringlet curls I'd pined for, ever since I was six years old and begged my mother for my first hot-roller set. My own hair could only be described by the endearing term "dishwater blond" and was so lifeless it looked like the "before" shot in a shampoo commercial. Between her curls and her full figure, Ruby looked like she'd stepped out of a Rubens painting. And this is what I thought every time I saw her—Rubenesque Ruby. It was wildly aggravating.

It wasn't really her hair that made me jealous, or because she was dating one of the Equity actors, or the fact she could drive nails in straight. It was because of her damned joie de vivre. Ruby was genuinely devoid of negativity and emotional strife. Ask her to haul out the garbage or sew four million sequins on a hat and she'd nod, honestly happy to be of assistance. Making matters worse was the fact that when she'd tried to shake hands the first time we'd met, I'd been too busy staring at her Disney princess hair to see her hand extended. Finally I'd noticed the expectant, then confused look on her face, pieced together what had occurred, and looked down just as she was lowering her wilted palm. Now, even though she was perfectly civil, I knew she thought I was a whopping asshole. Of course, being so magnanimous, she bore me no ill will, just felt sorry for my sad little shriveled-up heart.

"That's not why you should feel sorry for me!" I wanted to shriek every time I saw her, but it was too late to clear things up now and besides, she was right: my heart was shrinking down to a Grinchish size.

Not so long ago, I'd been a perky, capable girl like Ruby who— apart from the Frog Legs episode—had no reason to be anything other than sunny and optimistic. But ever since my visit to Dr. Hall, I'd been in the thick of a metamorphosis.

During my first few weeks at Williamstown, I just felt empty. My heart was like a vacant apartment that those chirpy roommates Joy and Hope had moved out of. By midsummer, the new tenants showed up and they were motherfuckers. Fear and Anger stomped around my insides, making renovations I hadn't approved—ripping up the floors, knocking down support walls. It wasn't just fear of the future that plagued me, but terror about what could befall me at any moment. Now that I knew how much of the picture I couldn't see, I felt skittish all the time. Was there someone silently standing at my side? A car speeding through my ever-widening blind spot? Fueling my fear were the accidents that happened constantly—banging my forehead into an open cabinet, twisting my ankle when I missed a stair.

I wasn't just scared, but mad as hell. I felt victimized at every turn, like I was perpetually getting the fuzzy end of the lollipop. Why didn't Rubenesque Ruby get struck blind instead of me? Now Ruby and all the other shiny, happy people would get to realize their dreams and I'd end up on government aid in an assisted-living facility at the ripe old age of thirty, maybe forty if I was lucky. I bathed in self-pity, and the longer I soaked in it, the more parched I became of positive feeling. It's no wonder I had no friends.

One morning in August, I woke to the sound of the phone ringing in the dorm room I shared with another apprentice. On the other end was my sister Marisa calling from Italy where she was spending the summer with Aunt Rita, my mother's sister. I heard the clatter of cutlery being laid, and Italian mothers calling across the piazza for their kids to come in for lunch. It sounded warm and lively and inviting. I felt like the Little Match Girl slowly freezing to death on the wrong side of the window, watching other people have a perfect holiday.

"You should get out of there and come to Italy," my sister said. "Aunt Rita offered to pay for your flight."

"It's not that easy." I sighed. "I'm locked into this."

I'd been raised with industrial-strength stick-to-it-ness. I'd never so much as quit a cup of tea halfway through drinking it.

Later that day, I stood in the wings ready to dress another actress for her moment in the spotlight, listening to the dialogue of the Arthur Miller play onstage and daydreaming about Italy. I hadn't been since I was a kid, when my grandmother took me to Priverno, her hometown near Rome. For years, I'd wanted to go back, travel the country, see the canals of Venice, but it was always too expensive or my summer was too booked with internships and part-time jobs.

Then I remembered I was going blind. If I waited, I might never see Venice.

In the middle of my reverie, I heard the line of dialogue that signaled it was almost time for the costume change I was helping with.

"You can only hope that you live with the right regrets," intoned the lead actor.

I'd heard that line every night for weeks. But tonight, it sailed right through the clutter of my mind and struck bull's-eye.

I'm not the sort of deep-thinking person who often has revelations but waiting in the wings, I had a Big-Bang-sized epiphany.

Carpe Fucking Diem.

Taking the safe, sensible route—finishing my tour of duty in this place I hated—was the wrong regret.

I'd tell the program director the next day that my great-grandmother was ill and I had to leave immediately for Italy. It was a lie and I didn't care. Let Ruby take my place hammering nails; she had a whole lifetime to travel and naturally curly hair to boot.

I, however, would throw caution to the wind. The way my father had attempted to when I was eleven and he pulled into our driveway on a Honda Nighthawk motorcycle.

"Oooooh," I'd shrieked, running to meet him at the front door, "Mommy's gonna kill you."

He hadn't returned that bike, like I thought he would. No, the Nighthawk had stayed; it just stayed parked in our garage. There was only one time that he took the bike out for a proper spin, crossing borough lines.

"I'm going to drive my motorcycle to work today," he'd remarked at breakfast.

"Over my dead body," my mother had remarked back.

They went back and forth while eating Raisin Bran, and finally reached a compromise. My dad would ride the motorcycle, and my mother, sisters, and I would follow him in the car, though the safety benefit of this is still unclear to me. I guess if he wrecked, she wanted to lock eyes with him as he flew through the air to meet his Maker so he could see those eyes shouting, "WHAT DID I TELL YOU, GODAMNIT?"

My sisters and I cried the whole way, and at red lights, we'd stick our heads out the window and shout, "Get in the car, Daddy! We don't want you to die!"

Soon after, the motorcycle was parked in front of our house, wearing a FOR SALE sign.

I thought of this story as I stood in the wings, plotting my escape from the theater festival.

This is my Nighthawk, I thought, *but I won't keep it all locked up. I'll ride fast and hard. I'll ride 'til the wheels come off.*

Within a week, I was kneeling at St. Peter's, my face suffused with the sunlight that poured through the stained-glass dove above the altar. I sat in Piazza del Duomo, taking in the majestic glory of the cathedral while drinking a Campari paid for by a handsome stranger, who just so happened to have a seat waiting for me on the back of his motorcycle if I felt like a ride. Not a Nighthawk but close enough.

I used the birthday and graduation money I'd been saving and blew it traveling through Vienna, Budapest, Amsterdam, and Paris. I drank in the sight of winding canals and towering palaces and smoking-hot international guys who didn't speak English, but didn't need to do any talking, anyway. I stood in front of Sacré-Coeur while its bells tolled and watched women on stilts waving scarves, and the undulating violet blur of the scarves against the white of the church and the blue of the sky made my heart ache with fullness. That was the right regret.

Dr. Hall was right. I did need to start making changes.

Life was telling me to find myself some silver linings. And to Life I said, "Don't mind if I do."

Tip #4: On smoking

Never light your own cigarette. You risk revealing your hidden handicap when you keep on missing. If you're showing a little décolletage, there's always a guy with a match nearby. Do it right and asking for a light can be alluring, very Bogart and Bacall. Do it wrong and it's still better than lighting your hair on fire.

4. NOTHING VENTURED

On those long train rides around Europe, I had plenty of time to ponder, and the more I thought about it, the more I realized how much I'd taken my vision for granted over the past nineteen years. I'd wasted a ton of precious time looking at the same faces, the same street signs, the same insides of the same rooms. Everything would change now that I had to cram a lifetime of sights into the next decade or so. I needed to accumulate images.

In order to see more, I'd have to do more. And in order to do more, I'd have to become someone different. Now that my eyes had been given an expiration date, there wasn't time to waste being a dishwater blonde with a good head on her shoulders.

I'd always been so cautious, sensible. "Better safe than sorry" was my family's motto, and the phrase I'd heard more than any other growing up was, "Be careful!" My mother and grandmother repeated it with a cultlike persistence, pairing it so frequently with "I love you" that to this day I find it hard to divide the two. Being careful all the time ruled out not just recklessness and spontaneity but, to a large extent, frivolity. Thus, my mother's idea of a good time was eliminating redundancies in the cereal shelf ("Why, WHY do we have two half-eaten boxes of Corn Flakes? Let's just *consolidate* them!"). All of my father's hobbies fell under the category of "things I'd pay other people to do," stuff like retiling the bathroom and washing the mop. Letting loose in our house meant pouring yourself a cup of OJ straight, not cut with water. When we went on vacation, my parents planned and attacked our leisure with such intensity that it was almost indistinguishable from work; we always beat the crowds to the beach, always preplotted our route through Great Adventure, never went to a restaurant that wasn't researched beforehand. And I'd always done the same. But not anymore.

Now I'd live boldly, like there was no tomorrow. On the plane ride from New York to Rome, I'd spent hours composing a big, sprawling bucket list, enumerating the many things I wanted to see before Lights Out. Top on the list was The Eyes of My Children, but that was one that would have to wait. Below that were a slew of travel destinations, many of which I reached that August—the canals of Venice, the Champs-Élysées, the royal palace of Vienna— and many farther flung. Then, too, there were plenty of items, each one more impossible than the last, that weren't so much things to see as ways to be, such as: Always Stop to Look at Sparkles in the Sidewalk and Sleep Only When Strictly Necessary and Read Absolutely Everything.

Sticking your nose in a book might seem like the very opposite of grabbing life by the balls, but reading had always been one of my great loves, and it was one of the things I was most terrified to lose. Sure, there were always audiobooks, but the holy communion of bringing your eyes to paper and sweeping them across the page, left to right, left to right, left to right, the rhythm of that dance, the quiet of it, the sound of the page turning, the look of crinkled covers stained with the coffee you were drinking when you read that chapter that changed your life—you didn't get any of that when listening to an audiobook, and I wanted as much of that as I could get, while I still could.

I didn't quite manage to read absolutely everything that August, but I did read absolutely all of *Anna Karenina*. And like magic, the reading of that book gave rise to real-life adventures. In particular, romances.

I was sitting on a bench next to a streetlight in Rome's Piazza Navona one evening, reading the chapter where Vronsky follows Anna to St. Petersburg, when I heard a man's voice next to me.

"Oh, that's a good one." The voice spoke in flawless English, with just enough of an Italian accent to be alluring.

I looked up and saw a thin, olive-complected man who seemed to be in his late twenties standing over me. It was nighttime so I couldn't quite make out the color of his eyes but they were dark, like his lashes and his hair, cropped short. In his clean, unwrinkled guayabera, with the Fontana dei Quattro Fiumi behind him, he looked like he was on a photo shoot for a spread in Italian *Vogue*.

"Are you a lover of Tolstoy?" I said in what I hoped was flawless Italian, with just enough of an American accent to be alluring.

An hour later, we were sitting at a two-top at Bar della Pace, drinking *vino rosso* and discussing Russian novelists. The tall, dark stranger, Benedetto, a doctor of philosophy in the field of medical bioengineering, hailed from a little town outside of Venice and was in Rome just for the night, taking care of some business related to his degree.

It occurred to me that I might have found the man not only of my dreams, but of my parents' too. After he'd paid for our drinks, I waited for an invitation back to his hotel room (which I was pretty sure I'd decline since even handsome doctors of philosophy can be serial killers), but no invitation was issued. Instead he insisted on walking me to the door of the apartment where I was staying with Aunt Rita, Marisa, and my cousins. In the cobblestoned alley in front of the building, he handed me a slip of paper with his cell phone number, urged me to call him in a few days, and then pressed his lips to mine in a gentle, lingering kiss.

I succeeded in waiting two days before calling him, which I

thought demonstrated pretty spectacular self-control. He was not just a gentleman, but an Italian gentleman, and those are the rarest breed. So when he invited me up north, to his hometown near Venice, it didn't take much deliberation before I agreed.

"But you don't even know who this guy is," Marisa pointed out the night before I left, licking the *panna* off the top of her gelato. She was seventeen, two years younger than me, and even less accustomed to reckless abandon: "What if he's a psycho who traps you over there and, you know, makes a coat out of your skin?"

I licked the last bit of *nocciola* out of my ice-cream cone and took a bite: "I highly doubt it. I mean, he didn't even try to lure me into his hotel room or anything."

"Yeah but he probably doesn't bring his torture equipment along when he travels," she reasoned, "so that doesn't prove anything."

This was a fair point. But had I or had I not just been diagnosed with an incurable disease that would soon leave me blind? Had I or had I not resolved to carpe fucking diem? Wasn't Find Great Romance one of the items of my newly composed bucket list? Nothing ventured, nothing gained.

"Well, I'll give you his number and address," I told my sister, popping the last bite of cone into my mouth. "And if you don't hear from me by midnight tomorrow, call the police and explain everything."

Benedetto did not have a dungeon in the basement of his house. He did not, in fact, have a house at all, or even an apartment, just an attic bedroom in his parents' place. His mamma washed and ironed his laundry and cooked dinner for him every night, including the night I came to visit. I sat at the kitchen table eating *spaghetti alle vongole* while his parents talked to him. About me, in Italian. Which I spoke, fluently.

"You, with the American girls," his mother lamented. "You can't find a decent Italian?"

"Look, I know what these foreign girls are offering you, and yes, a man should enjoy himself while he's young," his father chimed in, "while he still can."

"Oh-eh!" his mother chastised. "Watch your mouth!"

"But your mother's right, enough is enough!" his dad hastened to add. "Stop fucking around! Get your life together! Find a wife, not an American piece of ass!"

That night, in his bedroom (where I noted a glaring absence of Russian novels on the bookshelf), he put on a crappy pop album that had been wildly popular in the States the summer before and acted about as gentlemanly as a sailor on shore leave. It's not that I hadn't been looking forward to seduction, I'd just been looking forward to it being done well. His English, which had been impeccable when he was fabricating enthusiasm for Tolstoy, was not quite as fluent in the bedroom. Dirty talk, like cursing, is hard to do well when it's not in your lingua franca.

"Shit and balls!" he whispered. "You're a porn star!"

I was supposed to stay through Monday but when I woke Saturday, I told Benedetto my sister needed me back in Rome and I'd have to leave immediately. He dropped me off at the train station in Venice and after I saw him pull away on his Vespa, I headed in the direction of Piazza San Marco.

I spent a long, lovely day in the city I'd so longed to see, genuflecting before flickering candles in the Basilica, wandering down the labyrinthine alleyways, pausing to sigh on the Ponte dei Sospiri.

That evening, on the five-hour train ride back to Rome, I read *Anna Karenina* until my eyes ached. When I heard the conductor announce the end of the line approaching, I looked up from the book, disoriented, like I'd woken from a dream. It took me a minute to remember where I was and where I'd been, and then, I was happy, satisfied that my life was as full of adventure as the great novel I'd been reading. Yes, the last chapter, with my Italian beau, had been a bit disappointing, but it'd been memorable nonetheless and it had brought me to Venice, the city I'd always dreamed of seeing. My story was changing; no longer a maudlin tearjerker about a girl gone blind, but a broader narrative of youth and adventure that was only just beginning.

Italy had been the antidote, not to my diagnosis, but to the sadness, fear, and confusion the diagnosis had elicited. I'd laid the foundation there for a new way of life.

Back in New York, about to start my junior year in college, I reminded myself to keep building on that foundation. I thought about it as I went back-to-school shopping in the East Village and bought faux snakeskin pants and red patent leather heels. I thought about it as I dyed my hair for the first time, highlighting it with streaks of Hollywood blond.

"You know those chemicals are terrible for your hair," my mother observed, turning to look at me in the passenger seat. I was leaving for New Haven in a few days so we were running errands and had gotten caught in traffic on the Brooklyn Bridge, just the two of us in the car.

"It's just highlights," I said, fiddling with the radio that my parents had perpetually set to 1010 WINS. "It's not a big deal."

My mother blew her nose. Then she said: "Did I ever tell you I used to have epilepsy?"

I let go of the radio dial and looked at her. Now she was applying barely there lipstick in the rearview mirror.

"What are you talking about?" I asked. I figured she'd misspoken. She probably meant eczema or something.

"When I was a little girl. I had seizures all the time, every day," she went on, twisting the lipstick tube closed. "In the middle of school. Everywhere. They were really very bad. My teachers would call your aunt Rita out of class because she knew how to hold me so I didn't get hurt."

I sat there, agog, for once hanging on my mother's every word.

"Was this in Italy or after?" I asked. My mother had been born in a small town outside of Rome and had immigrated to America with my grandmother and aunt when she was eight.

"Both," she said. "It got worse when we moved to Brooklyn, when I was in junior high."

How could I not know about this? How had she managed to keep the single-most interesting fact about her childhood under wraps for nearly twenty years? Why had my grandmother or aunt never mentioned it?

"I couldn't lead a normal life," my mother continued, staring at the unmoving traffic in front of our car. "I really wanted to be a cheerleader but I couldn't even try out because I might have a seizure in the middle of a game. I didn't think I would be able to drive."

"So what happened?" I asked like a kid listening to a bedtime story. This was the first time my mother had delivered a monologue that did not feature the word "goddamned" or "moron" anywhere in it. This was engrossing stuff.

"One day, when I was about thirteen, I made it through a whole day without having a seizure. And then the next day, too. A whole week passed with no seizures. And that was it. I never had a seizure again."

"What do you mean?" I asked. "How were you cured?"

"That's what I'm trying to tell you. I don't know how. No one knew. One day, I just didn't have epilepsy anymore." She waited a beat before saying, "It was a miracle."

Ahhh. Now I understood the point of the story. But just to be sure, my mother spelled it out.

"Miracles do happen," she said, looking at me with welled-up eyes. "And you'll get a miracle, too. I know it."

I realized with no small amount of surprise that this crazy, out-of-the-blue pep talk had actually made me feel better. A lot better. Hopeful.

Later, at a computer at the library at school, I researched "childhood epilepsy" and found out there is a strain of the disease that corrects itself, usually before puberty, but this didn't contradict my mother's story about being the beneficiary of a miracle. One day she was biting her tongue on the classroom floor, and the next she was perfectly, entirely well and would never be sick like that again. That's a miracle no matter what scientific explanation there is for it.

We never discussed the childhood epilepsy again. I don't know if my sisters know about it, or my father. I've never even thought to ask them. I did wonder for a while afterward if maybe she really shouldn't have told me sooner, if maybe that wasn't exactly the sort of information the doctor meant when he asked the routine question, "History of epilepsy in your family?" Of course, since it was corrected, she probably figured it wasn't relevant. And since it wasn't relevant, it was easy enough to snip right out of her story.

I could understand that. A similar phenomenon was occurring with my own sickness, which didn't belong to my past but to my future. Something magical had happened while I was having adventures in Italy; my eye disease had been lifted out of the present tense, had been gathered together, all the loose ends tied up, and flung far, far down my time line, beyond the vanishing point of my distant future. Now, it was as if someone had gazed into a crystal ball and told me that in ten to fifteen years, I'd suddenly be struck blind. It would happen at some point but it wasn't happening *now*.

What made this possible was the fact that over that long, eventful summer, my eyesight hadn't gotten any worse. Not as far as I could tell, anyway. Intellectually, I knew that the deterioration of my retinas was slow, largely imperceptible, and that the steady elimination of my visual field happened even when I didn't notice it. Of course, intellect, particularly in teens, is exceedingly easy to ignore. All that mattered to me was that in September, I could still see as well as I had in June, could still read my copy of *The Unbearable Lightness of Being*, could still sew buttons on my pants, could still make out a professor's scrawl on the white board if I sat in the first few rows of the room.

Nothing was different—at least, with my vision. Which was funny because all the rest of me was changing, more and more every day.

I returned to college looking very much the same, seeing very much the same, but in the midst of a personality makeover. Of course, the transformation didn't happen overnight; learning to make bad decisions and do stupid shit, like anything else, takes practice. I got the ball rolling the way any nineteen-year-old would, in the bedroom. If your destination is Life in Living Color, it goes without saying that the fastest shortcut is the Indiscriminate Sex highway. My experience in Venice had proved to me that if I wanted to "Find Great Romance" I couldn't sit back and leave it all up to the men. If you want something done right . . .

In the beginning, the whole thing was pretty clumsy. My inaugural attempt at seduction targeted a cute freshman who was hanging lights for a Mamet play I was rehearsing. My roommate and best friend Beth masterminded the affair, so that all I had to do was follow the script she laid out. At her coaxing, I called him one night and invited him over and at her suggestion, I answered the door in a red teddy and knee-high leather boots.

What the hell do I do now? I thought, as the flannel-clad freshman looked around nervously, probably wondering the same thing. Beth hadn't scripted this part. So I regurgitated phrases I'd seen in movies, wincing internally as I said things like, "Glad you could make it," while lighting the wrong end of a Dunhill. I'd left the lights off in my room to create an atmosphere of romance, but it ended up backfiring when I couldn't see jack and nearly lit my hair on fire. Of course, the promise of no-strings-attached sex is so blinding to a teenage boy, the freshman probably wouldn't have noticed had I set *his* hair on fire.

Afterward, I was very pleased with myself. I was taking life by the horns, becoming mistress of my own destiny. I called the shots, not some eye disease.

Screw you, Dr. Hall, I thought, *I'm making changes but not the kind you had in mind.*

Just like that, before you can say, "woefully self-deluded," I'd persuaded myself that casual sex was a crucial part of my Carpe Diem strategy.

The rest of my college career was filled with brief dalliances each pretty much indistinguishable from the next, save for a tiny detail, some small remembrance—listening to "Blue Eyes Crying in the Rain" for the first time while a Texan made breakfast; the chiseled biceps of a King Crab fisherman; opening a gift box containing silver earrings brought back from Barcelona. These moments were little shards of color and if you put them all together the right way, I thought, they'd make a mosaic showing a grown-up, gutsy girl living life out loud, a girl who didn't take orders from a fat doctor on Park Avenue.

The whole idea was, of course, bullshit. I was doing nothing more bold or original than any other college coed does, desperate for attention and distraction—just tarting up, plain and simple. Still, I loved my new-and-improved persona. I loved being the kind of ballsy broad who wore geisha red lipstick and skirts short enough that you could catch a glimpse of garters. I loved cursing like a sailor, adopting pets without asking my roommates first, taking late-night skinny dips and generally undertaking asinine antics that would make my parents gasp, just because I could. Still could.

All of it was so terrifically exciting, I hardly ever thought about my eye disease, except every once in a while, and then only to convince myself that the diagnosis might just be the best thing to ever happen to me. It had woken me from complacency, given me a new lease on life and all without me actually having to grapple with any real consequences because my vision was, as far as I could tell, untouched. And since I wasn't thinking about the disease, and it didn't really affect me in any way, there was no reason to tell anyone about it.

I'd shared the news of my diagnosis with a handful of people, my close friends, right after I visited the Park Avenue doc, while I was still reeling. But once I'd found the cloud's silver lining, I decided not to share the news with anyone else. I didn't want the awkward pep talks and looks of pity. I didn't want my tale of woe to undercut the sexy, coming-of-age story I was improvising.

Besides, who knew what the future held? By the time the shit hit the fan with my eyes, I'd be like, thirty, maybe even older. Ancient, in other words. Who knew if I'd even *live* that long? And anyway, it was personal. Sort of like how I didn't go around volunteering my bra size when I ordered a cup of coffee or announcing to my Introduction to Fractals class every time I was on the rag.

It wasn't like it was a *secret* or anything, I convinced myself. I knew about keeping secrets and *this* wasn't *that*. You had to protect a secret with lies, like when a wife of my dad's colleague asked my mother for her famous cheesecake recipe and my mother maintained she'd lost the index card. My mother knew precisely where that stained and crinkled index card was; she just thought the lady should do her own legwork if she wanted to be known throughout downtown Brooklyn for her prize-winning cheese-based confections. Yes, I reasoned, I knew secrets and this wasn't one. This was an omission.

For all we know, Anna Karenina had a hint of a lisp or suffered from a touch of hip dysplasia; Tolstoy didn't tell us about it because it simply wasn't relevant. Really, I reasoned, this was the same thing: an extraneous detail I could cut out of the story. For now, at least.

Tip #5: On mood lighting

When attempting a scene of seduction, create ambience and prevent accidents by availing yourself of mood lighting. Candles are the obvious choice, but not the safest, since chances are good that you'll knock one over while climbing into bed or toss your lace demi-cup right onto the open flame, thus setting the room ablaze, only not the way you intended.

Try a lava lamp instead.

5. TECHNICOLOR

"Are you *insane*?" my mother's voice rang out from the phone receiver. "*Circus* school?"

"Just for the summer," I assured her. I was sitting on my dorm bed amidst piles of Post-it-riddled library books, making a meal of Twizzlers and Cherry Coke. "Don't worry," I added, "I'm not going to *actually* join the circus."

"Well, what a relief," she answered, piling on the sarcasm. I heard her yell to my father, who was probably reviewing echocardiograms in his office down the hall, "GREAT NEWS! YOUR DAUGHTER DECIDED NOT TO JOIN THE CIRCUS AFTER ALL!!!"

Then she turned her attention back to me: "Let me get this straight. Your father and I have been killing ourselves, working like animals, to send you to the most prestigious college, just so you can graduate and go to—clown class? While everyone else in your class is clerking for judges and working at Goldman Sachs?"

I wasn't the first college graduate in my family—my father, the son of a plumber, had matriculated from a small college in Brooklyn and worked his way through medical school in Italy—but I was the first to get a name-brand diploma, which had been my parents' greatest dream for me since I was a zygote. One of my earliest memories is meeting a Yale student while on the N train from Bensonhurst with my mother. As I read a Nancy Drew mystery, my mother had bombarded the girl with questions about the application process, SAT test prep, and the price of textbooks.

"That's the best college, anywhere, and it is *very* hard to get into," my mother had explained as we watched the girl exit the subway car in Lower Manhattan. "But you're smart enough to do it. I'm already saving money for your tuition."

She'd delivered on her end—squirreling away money every month into a college savings account—and I'd delivered, first, gaining admissions, and now, readying to graduate.

This, my mother kept telling me, is why my grandmother had immigrated to America and worked three jobs—not including the seamstress work she took in on the side; *this* is why my mother had scrimped and saved—never taking those Club Med vacations, only eating out on special occasions—all so I could be a Big Shot. And now, just when three generations of hard work was about to pay off, I was going to throw it all away for clown class?

"Actually," I clarified, gnawing on a licorice stick, "I'll specialize in contortion."

"I'm hanging up before you give me heart palpitations again," my mother decided. "We'll discuss this after your finals."

My new lease on life was proving a real hardship for my parents, instigating an epic case of *agida*. They were befuddled as to where they'd gone wrong with me. I knew this because my mother asked me on a regular basis: "Where, Nicole? Where'd I go wrong?" I might have elucidated the reasoning behind my sudden commitment to hare-brained adventures, namely the Lights Out deadline I was working under, but I didn't want everyone to get all depressed again. Particularly since there was no cause for gloom and doom; I was having the time of my life.

The last two years of college had flown by and now I was at the end of senior year, about to graduate. After a summer adventure in

San Francisco, I'd be renting an apartment in Brooklyn with Beth, securing a talent agent, and pursuing my dream of stardom—which could be lucrative, too, I was fond of reminding my mother as she massaged away her tension headache. Before I graduated though, I had one last college play to perform in, a lesser-known David Rabe doozie in which I played an exotic dancer who gets thrown out of a moving car. Which meant: not only did I get to simulate coke-snorting and wear a stripper costume, I also got to apply immoderate amounts of fake blood. Could things get any better?

They could, in fact. Because starring opposite me, playing the guy who threw me out of the car, was David.

I'd seen David around—he was a Theater and English major, too—but hadn't actually met him until we were cast in the play. Both our characters appeared only in the first act so we ended up having a lot of downtime together backstage.

You couldn't ask for a better companion to kill an hour with every night. David was solicitous and attentive; he'd remember little things like the fact that Charleston Chews were my favorite candy and would just so happen to have one in his pocket. May not sound like much but when you're used to emotionally unavailable hipsters, this is the stuff that takes your breath away. I attributed David's thoughtfulness to the fact that he was a Southerner. I'd never been below the Mason-Dixon Line and as far as I knew, all the guys down there were just like David, raised to finish everything on their plate, wear their hearts on their sleeve, and never tell a lie. I imagined Tennessee, where David was from, populated with tall, dashing Ashley Wilkeses who remember your preferred type of candy and remind you where you left off in the riveting story of how your roommate borrowed your favorite jeans without asking.

But unlike Ashley Wilkes, who despite his many positive attributes is about as interesting as a piece of zwieback, David had a tortured artist dimension that shot his appeal through the roof. He smoked Chesterfields, drank black coffee in the morning and

Maker's Mark at night, and wrote lovely lyrical short stories in the style of William Faulkner. He'd read everything, the whole Western canon and then some, including all of James Joyce's novels, even *Finnegan's Wake*, which *no one* read, even the people that claimed they had. His sense of humor was deliciously dry. And he looked like he'd just stepped out of the Sweet Valley High books I read as a kid, six-four with sandy blond hair and sea blue eyes.

The one catch was that he was taken. David had a serious girlfriend who he was moving in with after graduation. And a guy this honest, this steadfast wasn't about to step out on his lady. Until he did one night, with me.

It was a few weeks after our play had closed, just before finals, and we'd gone out for a catch-up drink and ended up back in my dorm room, reading ee cummings poetry. There's no chance two college coeds start reading all those gooey, lowercase run-on sentences and don't end up tangled in the bedclothes.

The thing that shocked me wasn't so much that he kissed me hard on my mouth right in the middle of my reading "i carry your heart with me." What shocked me was that he told me he loved me.

"But you hardly know me," I pointed out. *Like why I keep the lava lamp on*, I thought.

The fact that he knew little about me was, in David's opinion, a minor point. He wanted to be with me. He needed to be with me. I was like the very air to him, necessary for life. Which made it really very unfortunate because he couldn't be with me. Not right now anyway. Right now, he was going back to his girlfriend Mary's dorm room before things got too hot and heavy. The heart feels what it feels, he said, but that didn't mean it would make him a liar and a cheat.

"Maybe in another time, another place," he offered before walking out the door, exactly like the protagonist in a romantic comedy does at the end of the second act, before the cheesy music montage.

What the hell was that? I wondered, sitting on the edge of my unmade bed as the door closed behind him. The confession of love had been so sudden and had been snatched back so quickly, it was hard to know what to make of it all.

It was a distinct possibility, I thought then, that this whole Take Life by the Balls campaign might be a form of denial, a cheap way to dope myself up so I didn't feel sad and scared. Maybe, just maybe, I was acting out like Helen Keller did as a kid, thrashing around and knocking everything off the dinner table. Possibly, it was time to grow up, make a lasting connection, something in the realm of, maybe, love.

It was a distinct possibility—just not one I was willing to entertain.

Screw David and his earnestness, I thought, *I am on the cusp of beginning my adult life and it is going to be blow-your-mind, not-intended-for-all-audiences, fucking fabulous.*

I mean, who wanted to piss away precious time staring at the same mug across from you at the same restaurant where you ordered the same dish every Friday night? Let David wither in the boredom of monogamy. I was crossing shit off my bucket list—mainly the same item over and over and over again, but still, all the same, making indelible memories, feeling alive! I was about to train as a circus artist in San Francisco!

"It's going to look great on my résumé, in the special skills section," I assured my mother as I packed my California-bound suitcases after graduation. "How many people have trapeze experience?"

"I'm developing an ulcer," my mother replied from my bed, folding a pile of T-shirts I'd tossed there. "An ulcer!"

I knew that the ulcer wasn't really about me choosing circus school over medical school; the real source of anxiety for my parents stemmed from the fact that their tunnel-sighted, night-blind daughter was headed three thousand miles away. But to my relief, they didn't mention my visual impairment, choosing to fixate instead on the fact that Berkeley was where all the "crazies" lived and did I pack my pepper spray? In fact, since the summer of my diagnosis, no one had said anything much about my disease. My parents and grandmother could tell I didn't want to talk about it—or maybe it was *me* who could tell *they* didn't want to talk about it. Either way, it made us all feel better to pretend the diagnosis had never happened.

At circus school, I was trained by a bona fide Shanghai Circus veteran. Master Liao. Every morning, the tiny, smiley man with an unbending will had me holding handstands, knocking out push-ups, and shaking on chin-up bars. By the summer's end, I was in total command of my body, with every muscle boasting a perfect attendance record. "Here!" chirped my abs. "Present!" went the glutes. I could touch my toes to my head while in a handstand. Won't get you a job but it is a pretty cool trick at parties. It was exhilarating to feel like I was so in control of my body.

I paid for my training by teaching clowning to the little kids enrolled in the circus school summer camp. The endorphin rush from my morning workout was matched by the high I felt in the afternoon when I was with the kids—sweet, preschool-aged, hippie offspring. There was a little Russian girl I babysat for sometimes; we'd sit on a blanket in Golden Gate Park and I'd French braid her long blond hair while she taught me how to say stuff like, "My name is Nicole and I love porridge" in Russian. The gig afforded me disposable income, and more importantly, the confidence to believe I might make a competent mother one day, even with my failing vision.

At night and on the weekends, I worked at a fair-trade coffee shop in Berkeley and rehearsed for an off-the-wall comedy whose leading man, Ollie, was my sorta-kinda boyfriend.

Ours wasn't a sweet romance like I'd shared with Frog Legs, or a tender union like the one I'd enjoyed, briefly, with David. This was a rocky, lopsided love. Meaning, I craved him with every ounce of my being and he . . . dug me to some extent. It was hard to tell where he stood on the spectrum of amorous feeling—somewhere beyond "like" for sure, but before "love," which would have required that he stop banging his ex whenever the opportunity presented itself. I didn't care much what terms I had him on though, because when I was with him, I felt alive, awake. The drama was consuming and the sex made me feel like I was in a romance novel, a real bodice-ripper. Lamps were knocked over. Roommates squirmed at the banging on the wall. It wasn't quite the Great Romance I'd vowed to find but it was greatish. Memorable, anyway.

One night, as I lay languidly against him in the bath, I broached the subject of my eyes. Tentatively, I told him I had this condition; that I couldn't see in the dark or out of the corners of my eyes. I told him about the fat Park Avenue doctor. I hadn't revealed the diagnosis to anyone in a year or two and was out of practice, so the whole confession was vague and rushed and as soon as I'd started speaking, I regretted it. He hmm-ed and uh-huh-ed but didn't say a word. A few days later, in the middle of a bodice-ripping sex scene, I accidentally elbowed him in the jaw.

"Fuck!" he yelled, grabbing his jaw.

"I'm sorry," I said, flushed with embarrassment. I was waiting to see if I'd be forgiven, now that he knew my extenuating circumstances.

"Well," he grumbled, "just be more careful." Then he turned back to the business at hand.

Either he hadn't heard me or he'd chosen not to hear. Either way, I shouldn't have told him. In this respect, he was right: I did need to be more careful.

Toward the middle of the summer, I stepped out of my front door one night to meet Ollie for dinner on Telegraph Avenue and I met my next-door neighbor for the first time. He was walking out of his front door at the exact same moment. Had it been a movie, we'd have locked eyes and fallen instantly in love.

But we couldn't lock eyes because he was blind.

Not a little bit blind, the kind you could hide, but wear-dark-sunglasses-to-hide-your-freaky-eyes-that-don't-work blind. Carry-a-cane blind. He looked just a few years older than me, in his late twenties, a large man with broad shoulders, so tall he had to hunch down when he stepped through his door frame. It was odd to see a man who looked that young and strong, imposing even, carrying a cane. It was odd, too, to feel a kinship with this stranger, like he was wearing an emblem that signaled we belonged to the same club. More than odd, it was unsettling. I didn't want to belong to that club. Not now. Not ever.

I stood motionless in the doorway, one foot inside my apartment and one out, feeling nauseous and panicky. Should I just creep back into my place and wait for him to pass? Or—wait—maybe he wasn't all the way blind yet, and he could see me, in which case my backing away would be unforgivable. Was I supposed to introduce myself? Was that patronizing? I mean, why should I assume he was sociable just because he was blind? Maybe he was a misanthrope. Maybe he fucking hated unsolicited introductions, just wished do-gooders would leave him alone. Did he have the same eye disease as I did? Had he fallen into a bucket of lye as a child? Could I ask him or was that gauche?

As I stood there, exposed and bewildered and depressed, my neighbor turned to me. Even without a super-keen sense of hearing—which he, no doubt, possessed—you couldn't miss the sound of my hyperventilating.

"Hi," he ventured, his face pointed a few feet to the side of mine.

"Hi," I replied haltingly. "I'm Nicole. I, uh, live next door."

His face broke into a smile. "Oh, you must be subletting for the summer. Welcome, welcome! I'm Greg." He had a musical voice, deep and smooth and appealing and he smelled good, too, the light aroma of aftershave wafting my way.

How does he shave, I wondered, *without slicing his face to shreds?*

I was staring at his cane, which he held pointing straight down to the ground at his chest, so I was able to catch sight of his hand as it let go of the handle and reached out to me.

I extended my right hand to meet it.

"Good to meet you," he said, gripping my palm firmly. "I hope you're enjoying Berkeley. It can take some getting used to."

We stood opposite each other for a few minutes and chatted; he gave me recommendations of good places to eat and tips about which mentally ill homeless people were harmless and which to steer clear of. He told me he worked in development for a film company, and I told him I was an actress.

"Well, it was great to meet you," he said, pointing his cane at a forty-five-degree angle as he readied to head out. "Listen, if you ever need anything, let me know. Or if you want to come by and have a cup of coffee and discuss movies, it'd be a pleasure."

It wasn't a come-on or anything, just a genuine, neighborly offer.

"Sure, okay. Thanks," I said brightly. "Thanks a lot."

I never took him up on his offer. In fact, when I passed him on the street, I mostly walked right by without saying a word. Yes, it felt wrong, like I was manually pushing the dial of my moral compass away from "Right and Good," dangerously close to "Damnation and Hellfire Await." But no matter how affable and attractive Greg was, no matter how well groomed and gainfully employed, he was a reminder of something I had gotten very adept at forgetting. Running into him threatened my buoyancy.

And what a bubbly, delightful buoyancy it was. Only two years had passed since my visit to Dr. Hall but I felt light-years away from the dismal, dark place I'd inhabited after my diagnosis.

Sometimes, when I was working as a counselor with the circus school kids, if it was a slow day the program director would let them have a turn on the flying trapeze and occasionally, I'd take a stab at it, too. Climbing up the rungs of that ever-narrowing ladder made my stomach lurch but I couldn't let a five-year-old show me up. And besides, I was making hay while the sun shone.

I'd stand on the platform almost sick with nerves, one arm reaching backward to the cable to keep from falling, and the other arm stretching forward, reaching for the bar, fingers shaking. Then, before I knew it, I'd be dropping, not falling but leaping into thin air, every muscle activated, every part of me awake. I could fly. With every swing, I was pushing back the darkness from inching any closer. With every swing, I was setting myself free.

I'd promised my father it would be okay and it was. It was better than okay. My life was now in Technicolor, bright enough for even my eyes.

Tip #6: On applying fake eyelashes

As a rule of thumb, the secretly blind should avoid all activities in which they are required to glue objects onto their face. This includes the application of fake eyelashes. At best, you'll stick the lashes on asymmetrically, making it look like one side of your face has melted. At worst, the black, feathery clump will land in the area between your lid and your brow, causing people to think you're under attack by mutant spiders.

Should fake lashes be an occupational necessity—as is the case with celebrity impersonators and actors specializing in mid-twentieth-century farce—simply enlist the aid of a colleague. This can be achieved by batting your real lashes and blaming your abysmal fine motor skills.

Then try to find an office job. You have enough problems without worrying about this shit.

6. NOT WITH A WHIMPER

It was hot inside that birthday cake, even in the bikini. Tight, too. I crouched low within its wooden frame, wondering what the difference was between jumping out of a cake in a bikini in real life, and pretending to, in an Off-Off-Broadway show. Art, I guessed. But mostly, the tips. I was doing this particular cake dance gratis, in the hope that the play would get picked up by producers and moved to Off-Broadway. I'd graduated college a year and a half before and had managed to get an agent and my Actor's Equity card, but that didn't mean I could turn down work, not even the unpaid, jump-out-of-cakes kind.

My share of the rent for our railroad apartment, perched above a taco shop in Park Slope, was covered by my receptionist job at an accounting firm, and with the cash I got tutoring middle schoolers, bartending a few nights a week, and visiting Nonny for Sunday dinner ("Here, take twenty dollars! What, am I gonna take money to my grave?") I was getting by well enough that I could perform for free.

I wiped sweat from above my lip and pressed on the outer corners of my eyes to make sure the fake lashes there were still securely adhered. Then I ran through the burlesque choreography in my mind, readying to kick the top off the cake with a silver sequined heel. Once the dance was done and the guy in the gorilla suit carried me offstage, I'd have just one more costume change and a final scene to get through before opening night was over. So far, so good. But, as they say, it ain't over 'til the fat lady sings. Or, in my case, 'til the blind lady maims herself.

I was worried, for good reason, about the blackouts. The play was a madcap farce from the 1960s, and what it lacked in substance, it made up for in costume design. With every new scene, I had a new costume and coiffure. This meant lots of sprinting across the dark, crowded backstage area to my dressing room and back onstage again, which is an equation for disaster when you lack both peripheral and nighttime vision. But I told myself that with enough preparation, I could handle it. I reported to the theater early every night, before the rest of the cast arrived, and practiced each transition until I could do them, literally, with my eyes closed.

Now it was opening night and I'd made it through nearly the whole performance without a hitch—the burlesque dance included. No trouble popping the cake top, no wardrobe malfunctions during the vigorous shimmy-and-shake that followed, no late entrance of the guy in the gorilla suit.

Almost there, I thought as I stepped out of the bikini and yanked on an organza gown for the final scene.

I darted out of the dressing room, pulling up the zipper on the gown as I ran. Squeezed past the prop table, felt my way around the birthday cake. A few more steps and I'd be stage right, just in time for my cue.

Except that suddenly, instead of moving forward, I was falling down. I'd crashed into something massive and heavy, just at the level of my knees, and though I was blocked from the knees down, I'd been moving with so much momentum, the rest of me went flying forward until my throat encountered what felt like a crowbar. I recoiled, gagging.

My first thought was that I'd been attacked á la Nancy Kerrigan by some ruthless rival who'd been hiding in the dark with a base-ball bat. But as I pulled myself back up to standing, groping for support in the darkness, I realized that it hadn't been a person who attacked me, but a mobility scooter. Specifically, the mobility scooter used by the male lead in the first act to get a huge laugh which, according to my calculations, was supposed to be parked way the hell over in the wings stage left by now.

What kind of an asshole can't be bothered to stow his props in their assigned location? I thought. *I'd like to give him a sharp blow to the windpipe. See how he likes it.*

Not that it mattered now. What mattered now was whether I was bleeding. I shot my hand to my throat. Though throbbing, it felt intact. Then I heard my cue. Shaking, I minced my way to the stage entrance and, taking a deep breath, strode onstage.

"La—"

The word wouldn't come out. It felt as though there was some-thing lodged in my throat, interfering with the production of sound. I cleared my throat loudly. The audience waited. My castmates waited. The pregnant pause stretched on, past its due date, but my windpipe still felt blocked and all I could do was clear my throat again. Now my fellow actors were looking worried, and the audience shifted in their seats.

Having learned at circus school that it takes repeating some-thing three times to make it funny, I cleared my throat again, ex-travagantly, as if this was a fully intentional comedic sequence. The audience tittered, and their laugh gave me the confidence to try my vocal cords again.

"Lance Weatherwax!" I exclaimed. "Whatever in the world are *you* doing here?"

After curtain call, while the rest of the cast rushed out of cos-tume, excited to start celebrating, I undressed slowly. None of my castmates had seen my fall or paid much attention to the hiccup with my lines but still, I seared with embarrassment.

The blow hadn't been just to my throat. It always happened the same way; I'd go days, weeks, or months even, without thinking about the encroaching blindness, until it almost felt as if the whole thing had been a long, drawn-out nightmare, and then suddenly, I'd be reminded. It was never a gentle reminder, either, but a full-on assault, like Fate was bitch-slapping sense into me.

You can run but you can't hide, Fate hissed. *This is not going away.*

It didn't help my morale that these reminders tended to happen in the theater, thanks to the industry's insistence on blackouts in between scenes. Everyone else just followed the trail of glow tape to exit and enter the stage but that pale illumination was worthless to me. In the blackouts, it was near impossible to get myself on and off the stage what with everyone else running around and moving the furniture that I typically relied on to orient myself in the dark.

Once I'd gotten tangled in a backdrop in the middle of a performance. Once I'd stepped right off the front of the stage. Often, I'd been frozen, stuck onstage, unsure where to go, until a puzzled set runner grabbed my hand and pulled me off. I felt like a piece of furniture someone needed to be responsible for moving. It would have been easier had I told people about my night blindness but I'd tried that once and the director had raised his eyebrows and said: "You're night blind and chose a career in the theater?" which embarrassed me into keeping my mouth shut in the future. It was hard enough to get, and keep, work without revealing that you needed special accommodations.

And now here I'd gone and nearly broken my neck on opening night. It was folly, I thought as I combed out my beehive, to keep pretending like this.

But since I wasn't ready to either quit or risk discrimination by confessing my limitations, my only option was to get royally pissed off. If Fate wanted a fight, I'd give her one. I applied war paint in the form of Russian Red lipstick and rouge. I suited up for battle with four-inch heels, a low-cut slip dress, and a black feather boa, which concealed the bruise purpling on my neck. As a finishing touch, I decided to leave on the fake lashes; they made me feel protected somehow, powerful. When I walked out of the dressing room, my heels struck the floor so hard I imagined the wood beneath my feet splintering.

On the walk over to the cast party on Jane Street, I stopped into a bodega to buy a pack of Marlboro Lights. I wasn't a smoker really, but I did keep a pack in my purse, mostly as an accoutrement. I'd found that I sometimes needed a minute to orient myself, especially when I entered dark spaces, and rather than just stand there blinking like a moron while my eyes tried to adjust to the lack of light, I'd taken to busying myself with a cigarette. It was a cover, and a good way to meet guys, too.

Unfortunately, on a recent trip to my retinal specialist, Dr. Turner, I'd learned that cigarette smoking depleted the lutein in my eyes. She wasn't real clear on what that was or why I needed it but she was clear on the fact that my retinas were already shot to shit and it was pretty idiotic to knowingly make them worse.

Dr. Turner was a big proponent of parsing out info on a need-to-know basis. This was one of the reasons I didn't much like her, since, as a patient with a functional brain, I preferred being granted access to my medical information. The other reason I didn't like her was that she had as much heart as the Wicked Fucking Witch of the West.

I'd started seeing her about a year or two after I was diagnosed and she'd prescribed a medication to help shrink edemas in my eyes that might be making my vision worse. Well, she explained impatiently when I asked, they weren't *exactly* edemas but edema-like formations. In fact, it was entirely possible the medication wouldn't be effective. And, she added, I might experience side effects such as tingling in my extremities, nausea, mild tremors, ringing in my ears, and the frequent need to urinate.

"Anything else?" I joked. "Any risk of bleeding out my ears or growing a tail?"

She didn't laugh.

I didn't take the medication.

At least, not right away. A few months after she prescribed it to me, I came around and started thinking that it was worth a shot, even if it was a long one and I'd maybe piss my pants in the process. So I called her and explained that I needed a new script, because the one she'd written at my last visit had expired.

"You never took the medication I prescribed?" she asked.

"No," I confessed. "But I'm ready to now."

"I don't understand," she went on. "Why didn't you take it in the first place?"

"You know, I'm not really sure," I told her, surprised. I hadn't expected to have to defend my decision. "I think I just figured it was a long shot and then all the side effects—"

"Those are all common side effects of any medication," she shot back. "That shouldn't have been a consideration."

"Maybe—" I replied, "maybe I just didn't want the daily reminder. It's easier, you know, to just forget about my disease, for as long as I can."

She was quiet for a second. I figured she was thinking of something uplifting to say.

"Listen, I'm not a mental health provider so I'm not equipped to deal with issues like *that*," she replied. "For that, you'll need to talk to a psychiatrist. All I'm equipped to do is assess what medications may improve your vision and prescribe them to you."

"I understand," I said, though I didn't. She was the one who'd asked me to explain myself and once I did, she made me feel like a head case.

"I guess I'm just a little frustrated," she continued. "If I were you and someone told me there was a pill that could help me see better, I'd take it."

And if I were you, I thought, *I wouldn't be such a callous bitch.*

"I *will* take it," I reminded her. "That's why I called. For the prescription."

She sent the script, and I returned to her office in three months to determine if there was any change in my vision. There was not.

"Well, at least we tried," she concluded.

You call that trying? I thought. And promptly switched doctors.

So the fact that Dr. Turner had issued me a stern warning about cigarettes was not only not a deterrent to smoking; it was almost incentive. It wasn't that I set out specifically to spite my mean ex-doctor or anything, but when I did light up—and it wasn't often, just once or twice a week—I would feel a certain satisfaction picturing how pissed she'd be if she could see me *totally* disregarding her medical decrees.

At the cast party, still irate from my backstage fall, I took two or three long drags on the Marlboro Light that the bartender had lit for me and when I exhaled, I imagined blowing the smoke directly in Dr. Turner's smug face. Then I stubbed the damn thing out, only half-smoked. I had the emotional maturity of a ten-year-old but I did retain a bit of sense, after all.

The champagne was flowing freely at the cast party and I was in no position to resist, so I partook, and partook, and partook, until it was hard to keep my eyelids open. That's when I should have gone home. Instead I called Gabriel.

Gabriel was a good-looking Colombian-American actor I'd met at an Equity open call near Times Square a few weeks before. He'd insisted I get a drink with him after the audition, and I'd consented, mainly because of his gorgeous eyes, which were the color of melted chocolate. Over drinks, he told me a sad, lovely story about how his soul mate, a cousin in Bogota, was kidnapped by a drug lord who she'd ended up falling in love with. Now, he was trying to put the pieces of his heart back together. Would I like to go back to his apartment in Hell's Kitchen and watch a Monty Cliff movie? I would indeed. When we left the bar, it was pouring rain, a summer deluge that had us soaked well before we made it to the subway. So we retreated to a dark corner under some scaffolding on Broadway and became that writhing, tangled pair of shameless kids to whom it is commonly suggested: "Get a room."

Unfortunately, that first night wasn't just the tip of the romance iceberg, it was the whole damn thing. The attraction fizzled fast. Gabriel's backstory was the most interesting thing about him and the sex, when we weren't rain-soaked and drunk, was the worst ever.

I knew things weren't going well when, one night as we lay on his futon mattress, he asked why I was looking at him like that.

"Like what?" I asked.

"Like you're a little girl and you need something from me," he answered. "It's freaking me out."

Not that this lack of depth distinguished him from the rest of the men I dated. The guys differed but the dalliances were always the same, and their defining characteristic was "casual."

I was hungry as hell for companionship but didn't have a lot of emotional currency to spend so I'd taken to popping into the dating equivalent of drive-thrus—cheap, fast encounters lacking in all nutritional value and making you feel sick and hungry again almost before you were done. But I'd gotten used to my diet and hardly noticed the gnawing in my gut anymore, telling me I needed a real meal for once, something that would satisfy.

Gabriel was a perfectly decent diversion. But he wasn't the ideal candidate to console me after my opening night mishap.

Unfortunately, one forgets these details after one drinks most of a bottle of champagne. I dialed his number from memory, since I'd deleted it from my phone. He told me to come right over.

"You look drunk," Gabriel observed, ever astute. "And hot."

Soon we were rolling around on his lumpy futon. Mostly, I kept my eyes closed but once, I made the mistake of opening them and then I saw Gabriel's face, large and grotesque, his mouth twisted into a crooked grimace that was collecting drool on one side. Everything about the scene was dirty and repellent.

Hail Mary full of grace

Without meaning to I was praying, in a whisper. Turns out, even á la carte Catholics will knock off a few Hail Marys when the going gets tough.

Pray for us sinners

It wasn't the first time I'd done it during sex and I was fully aware that it did not bode well. I was willing to wager that even zealots refrained from praying out loud during sex, especially while squeezing their eyes closed and lying limp like a corpse. Still, it settled my nerves. And Gabriel didn't notice, anyway. I finished the Hail Mary and repeated a response I intoned at mass:

Only say the word
And I shall be healed

Afterward, it took approximately two minutes for Gabriel to sail off into a deep, unencumbered sleep. I, meanwhile, felt restless, with no idea what to do next. I peeled off my fake lashes—the right one was half off anyway—and left them on the pillow next to Gabriel's face, hoping they'd scare the living daylights out of him the next morning. Picking the glue off my lids, I weighed my options. I had no interest in spending the night, but heading home to my empty bed in Brooklyn seemed even less appealing. So I settled for a smoke on the fire escape.

I had nearly a full pack in my purse after all, and besides, I was drunk and lonely and it was a very cinematic thing to do. Plus, Dr. Turner had told me not to.

I pulled on some panties and Gabriel's T-shirt, lit a cigarette after a few tries, and groped in the dark until I got to the window that led to the fire escape. The piece-of-junk window stuck, so I held the cigarette in my mouth and used both hands to yank it open. Then I stepped out.

Except instead of landing on cool metal grates, my bare foot kept going. It stretched through the night air, reaching and reaching for a surface to grip until I felt the balance tip and realized with sudden clarity that there was no fire escape below, just a four-story drop down to the asphalt.

Instinctively, I jerked my body backward, yanking my head and leg inside and grabbing the window molding with a splayed hand. The cigarette fell out of my open mouth and cascaded down to the street. A few feet away, Gabriel snored on, oblivious to the fact that I'd almost accidentally killed myself. Because, of course, the fire escape was out the other window.

As I panted at the open window, I felt the sickening relief that rushes in once you realize you've narrowly avoided death or paralysis. A few inches more and the balance would have tipped the other way and I'd be lying half naked on the pavement, waiting for an ambulance, if I was lucky enough to retain brain function. What was worse is everyone would think I'd attempted suicide. Because who accidentally falls out a fourth-floor window? No one would guess I was so blind I couldn't see whether or not there was a floor underneath my feet, not even the people who knew about my vision loss, not even my parents. No, the story would be that I'd jumped.

I'm not in charge of my story anymore, I thought.

Somewhere along the way, I'd ceased taking life by the balls and had settled for taking men by them. And now, not even that. Now, it was me being taken. Where was the victory in *that*?

Only say the word and I shall be healed
Say the word
Say

I wanted to scream, a shaking, animal scream that would make the skin around my mouth ache and leave me hoarse. I wanted to put a fist through the window. But I knew that would wake Gabriel and the last thing I wanted to do was hear his voice. Instead I found myself shaking all the cigarettes left in the pack into my hand and closing my fist around them, clenching my fingers until the nails dug into my palm. I did it over and over, mashing the cigarettes until the filters were decapitated and the papers torn so the insides spilled out. Then I stuck my hand out of the window and let it all fall, let the tobacco rain down on Fifty-third Street.

Tip #7: On falling in love

No accommodations are necessary. Love is blind, just like you.

7. LONGER TO YOUR HEART

Two days later, on Monday morning, I woke to the sound of the phone ringing. The clock on my nightstand read 9:30.

Crap, I thought as I sat up in bed. *Not again.*

The answering machine clicked on and I heard the voice of Martha, who I worked with at the accounting firm in midtown:

"You're not picking up, so I guess you're on your way in. Call me an optimist. But in case you're still at home, I'll give you some incentive to get your ass in here. You got flowers. Roses. Yellow. Not my favorite. Still, if you're not here in an hour, I'm seizing them."

Well that's a surprise, I thought, as I searched my drawers for a shirt that would cover my bruised throat, *I guess Gabriel's more perceptive than I gave him credit for. Maybe he understood what a shit show Saturday night was. Not that it changes much. Still, might be worth another chance.*

Unlike Martha, I've always been a genuine optimist. Often, this makes me an idiot, too—especially in matters of the heart.

By the time I got into the office, I'd decided on what I was going to say to Gabriel when I called to thank him for the flowers. Which turned out to be a waste of time. The flowers weren't from him.

"It's a long way to the Smoky Mountains, but longer to your heart," the card read. It was signed, "David."

What I felt then wasn't misguided optimism. It was hope. My salvation had arrived on the scene and not a moment too soon.

David had been popping up in New York at parties and shows ever since I'd moved back to the city after graduation. Every time, he had Mary on his arm and every time I smiled broadly and gave everyone hugs, while stabbing pins into the mental voodoo doll I'd created in David's likeness.

What kind of a selfish sadist, I'd think, *tells someone he loves them when he can't—or won't—follow through?*

Then I'd go sleep with some aloof hipster, in an idiotic and ineffective "that'll show him" gesture, and then I'd go home and write awful, angry poems about David's facial hair and what a douche bag he was.

Seeing David was just a total buzzkill. Since my visit to the Park Avenue doctor, I'd perfected the ability to anaesthetize myself, mainly by jumping from one drama to another without ever stopping to think. I liked being comfortably numb; more than that, I relied on it. So it pissed me off when David would pop up like some bogeyman and startle me right out of my reverie.

It was unsettling in the first place that he possessed the power to rouse such feeling in me. Why should I be jealous? I should be happy that he was happy because, hey, I was happy myself. Everyone had gotten what they wanted. I had more suitors than a deb at her coming-out ball and all the drama—both professional and personal—that my heart desired. And David had love, with someone he had chosen over me.

How nice for us both, I thought, as I fantasized about kicking him so hard in the 'nads he'd never have children.

Then, one day, just after I was cast as the birthday-cake burlesque dancer, I found out through the grapevine that David and Mary had broken up. It was for good; she'd already moved out of the apartment in Queens they had shared. So, naturally, I called the apartment later that night and asked to speak with Mary.

"Nicole?" David asked. "Is that you?"

"Oh, hi, David." I was breezy, ever-so-casual. "I just had a question for Mary."

"I guess you didn't hear," he said. "Mary and I broke up."

I tried to make my gasp believable.

"I had no *idea*," I gushed. "I'm so sorry."

"Well, thanks," he replied, "but, you know, it happens."

He paused, and I didn't interrupt but gave him the chance to gather his thoughts. After a moment he said: "I feel like this is a sign, that you called. I've been thinking about you."

Bulls-eye.

By the time we hung up, we'd set a time and place to meet for drinks. I was excited, though not in a girlish, butterflies-in-the-stomach way as much as a villainous, revenge-is-best-served-cold way. Now I'd have the chance to make David feel awful, the way he'd made me feel after his futile confession of love. I'd show him what a big mistake he'd made passing me over before.

Because, of course, it was too late for us. I wasn't the same girl David had fallen for back in college. It had only been a year and a half since we'd sat in my dorm room reading ee cummings poetry but a lot had happened; I'd graduated from kitten heels to stilettos, from Midori Sours to martinis, from boyfriends to lovers. I tended bar in the meat-packing district wearing midriff-baring shirts. Beth had moved out of our mouse-infested walk-up apartment and I'd filled her spot with a perfectly nice, total stranger I met on the bus. Almost no one I spent any real amount of time with knew about my eye disease, except for my family, and we hadn't talked about it in years.

I had built a nice, hard titanium shell around my heart and it wasn't so easy to break through. So I agreed to go out with David but if he thought I'd swallow any more of those sweet nothings he fed to me before, he was crazy. And though I would sleep with him without much ado, I wouldn't pretend this was an exclusive arrangement.

"You're different," he observed when we met at a bar on Ludlow Street.

"No shit." I laughed, not bothering to mask my derision.

Despite the fact that I was about as approachable as a razor blade, David kept asking me out and trying, with no success, to break through.

Until the day he sent flowers. That morning, he made a dent. That morning, after spending a half hour searching for a shirt that would cover the bruise on my throat from my backstage accident, after finding the empty cigarette carton in my purse and thinking of the fate those cigarettes had met, which had very nearly been my own, I was ready for a change. I called David to thank him for the flowers and he told me he had a proposition for me—a work-related one. He'd like me to play the lead in an indie film he'd written and was shooting in his hometown in Tennessee next month. He was moving back there, at least for the time being, and would fly me out for a week of shooting now, and another week in a few months. It was a love story—the movie, that is. The collaboration, on the other hand, would be strictly professional, he assured me. He knew I wasn't looking for anything more.

A month later, I was flying south on a discount-fare puddle jumper. David was waiting at the airport to drive me back to his parents' house, where the out-of-towners—myself and an actor friend from college named Paul—were staying. David wheeled my suitcase through a hallway lined with framed school pictures into his childhood bedroom. Model airplanes hung from the ceiling and piles of Marvel comic books in plastic sleeves filled the shelf behind the bed.

"You can sleep here, and Paul will be in my sister's old room," he explained.

"Where are you sleeping?" I asked, leaning back on the bed with what I thought was a potent air of seduction.

"On the couch," he replied.

"You don't have to sleep on the couch," I pressed, rolling on to my side to amplify my cleavage.

To which bald-faced advance, he laughed.

"You better get some sleep," he recommended, walking to the door. "I'm waking you early tomorrow to start shooting."

What the hell? I thought.

"Oh, and I meant to ask." David paused in the door frame. "You can drive, right? I'm leaving early to set up and I bet you'll want to do hair and makeup here, instead of on the mountain. So I'll leave you the keys to my mom's car?"

"Sounds great," I lied.

A little later that night, after I heard Paul shut his door and the TV turn off in David's parents' room, I sneaked into the living room. At least, I tried to sneak. I was about as stealthy as a drunk rhinoceros. It was pitch-dark in the hallway and as I groped my way through, I managed to knock every single one of those school pictures out of whack. Once out of the hallway, I followed the sounds of a crackling fire to the living room where David lay sleeping on the couch, his face illuminated by the light of the flames. He wasn't waiting up for me, all knotted up with desire, as I'd expected. He was conked out, with a *Lord of the Rings* blanket circa 1982 pulled up to his chin.

As I sat on the couch and watched him sleep, an unsettling warmth spread through my body.

He looks so peaceful, I thought. *Better not wake him.*

Instead, I "crept" back to my bedroom, knocking over a decorative vase in the process, and spent a good hour or two snooping around. I flipped through spiral notebooks filled with poetry David had written from the ages of eight to seventeen and sifted through a stack of birthday cards he'd saved from various grandparents. I found an envelope of photos from prom and some old programs from high school musicals he'd starred in. By the time David woke me in the morning for our first day of shooting, a small but inarguable crack had formed in my armor.

The crack on the siding of his parents' house when I backed the car into it the next morning—that wasn't so small.

"Honey, why don't you let me drive you over to the mountain," drawled David's mother when she heard the thud. "I don't mind."

The next few days were consumed with the film shoot. At night, David's mom would show up with dinner for the cast: homemade meat loaf and mashed taters, fried chicken and corn bread, pulled pork sandwiches with bottomless cups of tea so sweet it made my teeth ache. After we'd wrapped for the day, the cast would retire to a bar downtown where a gravel-voiced woman named Peaches would serve beers and bourbon and moonshine cherries. When we'd get home, nice and liquored up, I'd change into something a little more comfortable and visit David on the couch and every night, he'd already be asleep.

David had given me full access to his life—his past, his family, even his baby pictures—and, at the same time, had denied me access to him, mysteriously stopping his pursuit of me in its tracks. You couldn't craft a more powerful aphrodisiac. That he'd done it entirely by accident only intensified its power.

By the time we wrapped on the final night of shooting, the deal was sealed: David had sandblasted through my defenses. On that final night, as soon as we got back to his place, I went to him on the couch. I was still in costume, a flannel button-down shirt one size too big with Walmart jeans and no lipstick.

I sat on the couch and watched as he lit the fire and made the room go from dark to dancing in light.

"I'm glad you invited me down here," I said. "The South isn't what I thought it would be."

"No?" he said, closing the grate on the fireplace.

"Neither are you," I said. It was sickening to be so goddamned exposed, to have nothing to hide behind, but the alternative—leaving David, leaving the warm feeling and the firelight to return to fucking and falling out windows—was even more sickening.

David didn't reply but he sat next to me on the couch. Close.

I couldn't see much by the dim light of the fire but I could make out his eyes. They were looking right at me, inviting me in, not pushing it or reaching for it but just leaving the door open.

"I'm not really so cold-hearted, you know," I said, squirming from the discomfort of being so naked.

"I know," he answered.

I felt his hand then on my face, brushing my hair back and with that touch, the remains of the Great Wall surrounding my heart fell with a resounding crash. That night, he slept next to me and there, curled in the crook of his arm, I stepped out from where I'd been hiding and told him about my eyes, not just the disease and the prognosis but the secret of it, that I didn't want anyone to know and I didn't even know why. It was dark in the room so I couldn't see his reaction but I didn't need to because I felt his grip around me tighten.

After he kissed me good-bye at the airport the next day, he told me he loved me, that he had loved me for a long time, that he wasn't going to let me get away again.

When I returned to Tennessee two months later for the final week of the film shoot, David came into my bed on the first night. Afterward, as we lay tangled in Holly Hobbit sheets, he said he had to show me something.

"A surprise?" I squealed. "A present? What is it?"

"You'll find it," he told me.

I ran my hand over his chest, his left arm, then his right. There, above his tricep, was a bumpy patch that hadn't been there before.

"What happened?" I asked.

I heard him rustling with something and then the bedside lamp flashed on. I reached for his arm.

There, in raised, irrevocable ink, were six lowercase letters.

nicole

"I carry your heart with me," he said.

When my plane took off a week later, I wasn't on it. I stayed in Tennessee until David packed up his stuff. Then, together, we drove back to New York—not just for good, but for better and worse.

Tip #8: On driving

Just because you are in possession of a valid driver's license does not mean you should get behind the wheel. That would be like saying that just because your acid-washed jeans from high school still fit, you should wear them.

8. CALIFORNIA DREAMING

"You're joking," my mother challenged, slicing a milky mound of mozzarella. "I don't believe you."

I sighed loudly. Spending five minutes around my mother had a tendency to turn back the clock, reducing me to an eye-rolling sixteen-year-old again. And at twenty-four, it wasn't so far to go.

"I guess you'll believe me in two weeks when you show up at my apartment and find someone else living there," I told her. "Because I'll be in LA."

My mother sighed right back at me. It was Christmas afternoon and the last thing she wanted to be doing while preparing antipasto was discussing my cross-country move.

"This house is a pigsty," she sighed. "And everyone is going to be here in a few minutes."

The mess she was referring to consisted of a half dozen CDs on the coffee table that hadn't been returned yet to their cases, and my pair of leather boots, kicked off at the door, which were lying haphazardly instead of lined up in the closet. My parents' ultramodern apartment in midtown Manhattan was appointed all in white leather and glass and my mother prided herself on keeping it immaculate.

Not unlike Joan Crawford in *Mommie Dearest*, I was fond of pointing out. When I did, it always elicited the same response: "Me, crazy? Please! You haven't *seen* crazy!" Precisely the sort of thing, I observed, that only a crazy person would say.

"I haven't even had a chance to wrap any goddamned presents," my mother complained, gesturing with her knife at a bunch of shopping bags on the dining-room table. "Why don't you wrap some of that crap to go under the tree?"

I sat down on the banquette next to the table and unfurled the roll of golden wrapping paper that my mother has used to wrap Christmas presents for the past two decades. I'm not sure where she got her hands on the paper but the price must've been knocked down at least 80 percent because she purchased no less than two dozen rolls of it. It's like a magic trick; the golden wrapping paper just never ends. I am confident that it will last, literally, a lifetime. And if it doesn't and she finds one day that she's come to the last paltry patch, my guess is she'll outlaw Christmas.

"I don't understand," my mother went on. "What's in LA? All the big actresses live in New York."

I looked closely at the oversized pink pleather wallet I'd pulled out of a shopping bag.

"Ma," I said. "You gave this wallet to Marisa last year and she didn't want it. And the year before that, you gave it to me."

"She's right," my father said, coming down the stairs wearing jeans and a hospital scrub top. "Nobody wants that wallet."

"Then you're all a bunch of morons," she shot back, laying the sliced mozzarella in a neat, overlapping circle on a platter. "That is a gorgeous wallet! I had to rip it out of another lady's hands at a sample sale."

She glanced up from the platter, spotted my father, and shrieked. "Why the hell are you wearing those dirty old dungarees?"

"Dungarees" is one of those words my parents refuse to part with, despite the fact that no one else has uttered it since 1929. You could create the world's best drinking game based on how many times my parents use the term.

"These are my favorite dungarees," my father protested, taking a London broil out of the fridge.

"Why do we have to have the same argument every year?" she pleaded. "A homeless person wouldn't accept those dungarees! They'd be highly insulted!"

I reached in the bag and pulled out a three-pack of argyle socks.

"Those are for your cousin," my mother said, still shaking her head in disbelief at my father. "And don't forget to take off the price tag."

"Where's the scissors?" I asked.

"Over there," my mother replied, gesturing with her knife. By the time I'd followed the length of her arm to note where her hand was pointing, she'd dropped it to resume slicing vine-ripened tomatoes.

"Where, 'over here'?" I sighed.

"Right over there, on the table," she elaborated, nodding her head vaguely in my direction.

Precise, descriptive language was never my family's forte, which had become bothersome; the more constricted my field of vision became, the more I relied on descriptive language to help me locate missing items. While a normal-seeing person could just sweep their eyes swiftly and effortlessly over the table as a whole and locate the scissors within a second or two, it would take me five or six times that long, because I'd have to make five or six much narrower sweeps, covering one small section of the table at a time. Little hints like "to your left, next to the orchid" or "right near your elbow, by the window," would speed up the process considerably; but since I'd never told my parents I needed these hints, they didn't know to offer them. So I just sighed to myself and began my laborious hunt for the scissors, moving my gaze over the table like a spotlight from left to right until I'd found them, in the center of the table, on a stack of blank Christmas cards.

Meanwhile, my mother was catching my father up to speed on my travel plans: "Did you know your daughter wants to move to Hollywood? Are you aware of this?"

"What the hell are you talking about? Who's moving to Hollywood?" my father grumbled, massaging marinade into the London broil.

"I've already told both of you this, like, five times," I said as I cut a sock-sized square of wrapping paper. "All the TV work is in LA. Everyone moves there eventually. And it makes sense to do it sooner rather than later."

The last observation hung in the air, its intimation unfolding like a bad smell, curling around the room and making everyone's stomach clench. In a few years, I wouldn't be able to audition for the spunky best friend or the tough-as-nails prosecutor. In a few years I wouldn't be able to audition for anything except for the blind girl.

My vision had held up well in the four years since my diagnosis but I could tell it was slipping. I couldn't read the newspaper anymore. Finding the bathroom in dark bars was becoming a problem. Just last week, I'd chipped a tooth when I tripped over a planter on Wall Street. If I wanted to have a decent shot at becoming a big-time blockbuster starlet, there was no time to lose.

I'd explained all of this to David when I announced to him just a few weeks earlier that I was going to move to LA. We'd been together for a little over a year, ever since we finished filming the movie in Tennessee and drove back north together. Things between us were going well, unfolding at a comfortable, leisurely pace after an explosive beginning. David wore my name on his arm but that didn't mean he owned me. He had his own apartment a few blocks from mine, his own circle of friends. If David was hurt that I made the decision to move without consulting him, he didn't show it. In fact, after considering for a few days, he told me he'd always wanted to live in California and would come along.

But though I'd confided the full explanation for my move to David, he was the only one I was honest with. The closest I got to full disclosure with my parents was dropping the phrase "sooner rather than later" and the pause that followed was so tense, I decided to spare us all by offering the standard justification I was feeding everyone else.

"I mean, I could wait; I could spend a few more years auditioning in New York. But I'm at my peak now, and in LA, the younger you are, the better. It's like dog years out there—twenty-four is really thirty-four."

I pulled a meat tenderizer out of the bag.

"That's for Nonny," my mother said, looking up. "She broke hers."

"I already found an agent out there and a sublet off Sunset Boulevard. I'm leaving in two weeks to be there in time for pilot season," I explained, attempting to wrap the tenderizer neatly enough that my mother wouldn't go off on a rant about my subpar wrapping skills.

"So the only question is," I said, finally coming to my point, "can I have your car?"

My father, with a pepper grinder in his hand, piped up: "But you don't drive."

Oh for fuck's sake, I thought, *how did I know this would come up?*

"That's not exactly true," I protested. "I have my license."

I hadn't gotten it the first time I tried, when I botched Driver's Ed in high school. Once I was diagnosed with RP though, this mystery, like so many, was instantly cleared up. Of course I was a lousy driver; I had no peripheral vision. If I wasn't looking directly at something—the streetlight, the car trying to merge in front of me, the person crossing the intersection—I would have no idea they were there. Unfortunately, while I was busy looking directly at something—say, the red light I missed the last time I took the car out—I'd miss something else, like the car that had come to a stop in front of me.

The sensible thing would've been to resign myself to never learning how to drive. I lived in New York after all, and plenty of my friends who could see just fine never got their licenses. It's a point of pride for New Yorkers not to know how to drive. But I knew it would never be a point of pride for me.

So a year or so after my diagnosis, I decided to get my driver's license. Now that I knew exactly what my driving deficiencies were, I could compensate for them. My father took me to a deserted parking lot a few times and there, with no living creatures to plow down in cold blood, I pioneered an innovative driving technique for the visually impaired. What it boiled down to was turning my head from side to side a lot. Though my head-swerving style of driving made me look a bit loopy, it was not grounds for denying me a license—at least that's what the guy who'd administered the driving test had said.

"Just try to relax," he advised me as he signed his paperwork. "Look out of the corner of your eye."

"Oh definitely," I promised him. "I will."

Passing the eye exam wasn't hard, since with turbo contact lenses in, my central acuity was still pretty decent and the test didn't cover peripheral vision. So, with one-third the visual field of a normal person and totally night blind, I got my license—cause for celebration for me, and cause for widespread panic for the world at large.

But as my father was quick to point out, the fact that I'd duped some guy into giving me a license a bunch of years ago didn't mean I knew how to drive.

"Oh, David will teach me as we drive cross-country," I persuaded them. "I'll have plenty of practice on the interstate."

From his furrowed brow, it was clear that this was just what my father was afraid of. But he didn't say anything and neither did my mother. This, I knew, was a testament to their love for me, because ordinarily my parents have zero ability to keep their ocean of negative opinions from pouring out. My mother likes to talk about how she bites her tongue until it bleeds and I like to point out that if you're constantly communicating how much you're biting your tongue, you're probably not biting it hard enough. The subject of my eyes was the one area in which my family censored themselves and I knew they did it to spare me feeling upset or embarrassed. It was exactly the same reason I didn't bring it up with them.

"So what do you think?" I pressed, collecting and balling up the extra scraps of wrapping paper. "You don't need the car anymore since Marisa graduated and you won't get much if you sell it. And I'll be really careful."

I carried the excess wrapping paper over to the kitchen garbage but halfway there, I found myself doubling over something hard at my waist.

"Shit," I hissed. Looking down, I saw the metal handlebars of a step stool. Someone had been changing a lightbulb overhead.

"That was my fault!" My mother rushed over to fold up the stool. "I shouldn't have left the goddamned thing in the middle of the living room. Are you—"

"I'm fine," I barked, embarrassed. My hip bone stung from where I'd bashed it, but I straightened up and took the last few steps to deposit my garbage in the trash. When I looked up, I saw my father at the sink regarding me with sad eyes.

Not only did his look make me feel sad, it made me feel like a cause for sadness. Though I'd become pretty adept at tiptoeing around the land mine of The Look, occasionally I'd step right on it and then, it was as if all the things he kept himself from saying poured out of his eyes.

"My daughter," he said wistfully. "My daughter wants to be a movie star."

A week and a half later, the day after New Year's, I was shutting the trunk of my parents' Subaru Outback, or attempting to, since with all the boxes and suitcases and lamps and hot-roller sets, it would barely close. I kissed my parents good-bye, looking over my dad's shoulder to avoid his eyes.

Then I slid behind the wheel. As my mother would say, God help us all.

Tip #9: On pool parties

Avoid parties that take place around a body of water. If you must go, make sure there's alcohol present, not for you to actually drink—unless you have a death wish—but to pretend you have drunk. That way, when you fall in the swimming pool fully clothed, it won't look suspicious. It'll still look idiotic, just not suspicious.

9. HELL ON WHEELS

It took me exactly three days in Los Angeles to realize I'd made a colossal mistake. It was at that point that I started crying.

David was incredibly sympathetic, in the beginning. He'd sit next to me on the paisley couch of our sublet off Sunset and hold me while I cried, assuring me I'd get used to California if I only gave it a chance. After a day or two, he took to smoking on the balcony and gently reminding me that it was *my* idea to come to LA. After a week, his empathy depleted, he tried Tough Talk.

"You remember that I quit my job, got rid of my apartment and packed all my shit up so we could come here, right? To realize your dream?"

"I know," I wailed. "That's what makes it so awful."

"I just don't understand how you can hate it so much already."

"I have no friends," I choked out, "and there's no good pizza and"—I paused to catch my breath—"I'm trapped in this house because I don't know how to driiiiiiiive."

My father had been right: I couldn't drive and it wasn't as easy as I'd thought to learn. Though the idea of learning how to drive on our cross-country trip had sounded perfectly sensible when I explained it to my parents, it seemed considerably less so when I saw the eighteen-wheelers speeding beside us at eighty miles an hour. So I couldn't drive my cowardly ass back to New York and I didn't have enough money for a plane ticket. I was stuck in sunny, sweet-smelling, motherfucking California.

"Just give it time," David sighed. "You'll get used to it."

Which I did, seeing as I had no choice. It took a while but eventually, I had fully furnished my life in Los Angeles; I had a cushy long-term temp job at an investment bank, a go-to acting coach, a respectable amount of TV auditions. I knew where to get a halfway-decent slice of pizza, though an edible bagel was still beyond reach. I even made a handful of friends; not enough to pack a stretch limo but enough to fill the available chairs in my living room during an Oscars party. Yes, I had gotten used to LA.

The thing was, what I'd gotten used to was feeling like I didn't belong.

After two years, Los Angeles was thoroughly familiar to me but nothing like home. Home was the brick attached house in Benson-hurst with a Virgin Mary in the front garden where my grandmother could whip up homemade tagliatelle in fifteen minutes or less. Home was the long, bright expanse of Broadway, which was always blazing with light even in the wee hours, so I never had to stumble or even slow my step. Home was the rattling subway packed with all sorts of people—young, beautiful Hollywood types, sure, but un-kempt homeless people, too, puking in grocery bags, and fat middle-aged ladies who took up two seats and full-grown men who only came up to my waist. People missing legs and arms and hair. People with long, spindly white canes. The subway was a land of misfit toys, and I belonged there, even though I was only a misfit in se-cret. The subway would take me wherever I wanted to go, when-ever I wanted to go there. That was a freedom I'd lost, and I missed it desperately.

It's not that I couldn't drive. David had taught me how, once I'd finally stopped crying. We started out in the 99 Cents Store parking lot, then moved up to side streets, and finally, I graduated to the boulevards. After a month of daily practice, I was cruising down Santa Monica solo, singing along to the radio.

On the streets, I was an okay driver, below average maybe, but way better than someone who'd drunk a fifth of Jack Daniels, say, or a child. At the very least, I tried hard. Hence my idiosyncratic driving posture. When my sister Marisa came to visit from New York, she couldn't help but notice.

We hadn't even made it out of the airport parking lot when she piped up.

"Maybe—," she ventured hesitantly, "maybe you want to lean back a little."

"What are you talking about?" I snapped, concentrating on my left turn.

"You don't notice how close your face is to the windshield?"

It was true. My nose was almost touching the glass, my chest nearly pressing the wheel. Once or twice, my chest *had* pressed the wheel and honked the horn, which had the exact opposite effect of what I'd intended—to blend in. It looked like I'd been taught driving posture by an octogenarian.

"There's no law about sitting too close to the windshield," I shot back. "Just sit back and enjoy the ride."

I couldn't see my sister's face but I bet she looked like she was enjoying the ride about as much as a turn on the Tilt-A-Whirl with a stomach full of corn dogs.

My uncool driving style notwithstanding, I did a decent job of getting from point A to point B without dying or killing anyone. In general.

Of course, certain restrictions did apply.

There was a lot of fine print involved in my driving arrangement, lots of blackout dates. The gist of the arrangement I made with my-self was: Yes, I could drive. But then there were a whole bunch of exceptions. Interstates, for instance, were out of the question. State highways were pretty dicey, too, though they were impossible to avoid. As a rule of thumb, I tried not to drive the car more than thirty miles an hour since I knew it was a matter of time before I sustained a head-on collision and I figured when that occurred, thirty miles an hour would do less damage than seventy. The big trouble with highways was the merging. Merging is one of those skills that require a lightning-fast synthesis of visual information that is impossible for someone who can't look in front and to the side at the same time. Every time I picked up speed to approach the 101, I was making a Hail Mary pass.

So, judicious highway usage. Zero drinking and driving; that was just pressing my luck. No driving precious cargo, like kids or pregnant women, because there was no way to ensure I wouldn't kill them. But that was all really pretty easy, little stuff.

And then there was: no night driving.

This was an absolute deal breaker. This was: eat anything in the garden you want, but leave that apple tree alone. In my world of partial-sight there was a lot that was negotiable, a lot of borderline situations. But this was black-and-white. If I wanted to avoid bloodshed, to say nothing of having my secret outed, sundown was my deadline. Full stop.

At first, it didn't seem so hard a deal to stick to, but neither did forgoing that one lousy apple tree. It soon became clear that not being able to drive after dark would make life complicated—at the least robbing me of independence, at the worst leading to entanglements that were, well, compromising. Like ending up in the hot tub with the King of Candy.

It was one of those situations for which there is a perfectly reasonable explanation that ends up sounding a lot like an excuse, one of those situations where you find yourself blaming everyone and everything except for yourself.

In a way, it was LA's fault.

There are an unreasonable number of swimming pools in LA.

People who live in homes with pools feel compelled to throw parties centered around them. These parties, like most, take place at night. As an actress, I had no choice but to go; that's half the job, the other half being split evenly between Botox and dieting. Unfortunately, as a night-blind person, I didn't belong around deep bodies of water, especially in four-inch heels which, let's face it, are mandatory in Hollywood. On a penumbral pool deck, one of the safest places for a girl like me is sitting inside the hot tub. Unless you're sitting with an octopus-armed guy who won't take "no" for an answer.

So in a way, it was the fault of Los Angeles. In another way, it was Kat's fault for running off to schmooze with that hot, young casting director and then disappearing into the crowd.

Kat was my best friend in Los Angeles, a rare beauty of ambiguous ethnic origins, which was useful casting-wise because she could audition for everything from Sacagawea to a Bangkok hooker. Her lips were so supersized, more than one woman on the street had begged her for the number of the genius who'd done her collagen, only to discover that her lips were, like almost nothing in Hollywood, 100 percent real. Her lustrous, ebony mane bounced around so dynamically, it looked like it had its own blood supply. Most maddening of all was that Kat was as smart as she was telegenic. She'd graduated summa cum laude from Yale, where I'd met her years before we ran into each other again in Los Angeles, and her fallback career if acting didn't pan out was high-risk corporate finance. Besides being smart and connected, she was loyal and funny, all of which made her a great friend, even though standing next to her in public frequently made me want to kill myself.

Not only had Kat been my ride to and from the party, she'd also been my ticket in; she knew a guy who knew the guy who was housesitting at the exquisite home overlooking Sunset that was packed with industry people—mostly actors with a few agents, directors, and casting people tossed in to start a feeding frenzy. The house was massive; the pool deck alone was bigger than the three-bedroom apartment I'd shared in Brooklyn. Chateau Marmont was just up the street and I overheard someone pointing out that you could see Tobey Maguire's deck from the bar.

I'd guessed what kind of a crowd it would be, which is why it had taken me nigh on two hours to get ready. After painstaking deliberation, I'd settled on wearing a pair of tight jeans and heels with a shirt so insubstantial it would be better characterized as a handkerchief. Despite its size, and the fact that I'd found it on the half-off rack, the shirt had cost a pretty penny at the Robertson boutique where I'd purchased it a few weeks before. I didn't want to ruin a shirt like that. So, naturally I took it off when I got in the hot tub.

It didn't seem like such a big deal. Which is to say, everyone else was doing it. After two years in LA, I'd come to see this as a perfectly legitimate defense, a fact that's not surprising when you recall that trying to make it as an actress in Los Angeles is exactly like trying to survive high school. I could almost hear my mother inveighing, "If everyone else jumped off the Brooklyn Bridge, would you?" but I'd left my mother, along with my good judgment, in New York. Checking your self-worth and decency at the door wasn't just an occupational hazard as an actress in LA; it was an occupational necessity.

Besides, I justified to myself, it wasn't like I was going to do anything stupid, like sleep around on David, who was waiting at our place in West Hollywood. He refused to come along to these industry parties, found the whole racket deplorable, and nothing I said—or wore—could persuade him to trade in a night of beer, peanuts, and zombie movies for shameless networking. David wasn't prone to jealousy and he felt reassured when I went out with Kat because she, too, had a serious boyfriend who she'd never cheat on, no matter how much she flirted. Yes, Kat and I served as expert cock blocks, swooping in to save one another before push came to shove.

So where the hell is she? I wondered as I steeped in the hot tub, squirming away from the King of Candy's arm.

He wasn't the King, in point of fact, but the Prince, heir to the kingdom. His father owned the company whose chocolates were responsible for my freshman fifteen back in college. The King of Candy belonged to the only other category of people who came to these parties apart from Industry People, and that was Filthy Rich People who Know Industry People. I'd met him in the gazebo, where I'd taken refuge after Kat wandered off, because it was the only spot on the deck that was at all illuminated. I'd almost fallen into the pool a few times already and though I'd prepared an excuse should that occur—*Shit, I should've stopped after the third drink*—it would really be better if I didn't.

So I'd taken my chardonnay over to the gazebo and arranged myself carefully on a stack of silk pillows there, hoping I'd look Too Cool for School rather than Too Blind to Party. It must have worked because a few minutes later, the King of Candy introduced himself and ever since, I'd been asking him detailed questions about candy production and laughing my head off like an idiot. It wasn't that he could advance my career or anything, like Kat's catch, but talking to him kept me from being a wallflower and I'd pay any price to avoid looking like I had no one to hang out with. Including following him into the hot tub.

There were a dozen of us in the Jacuzzi and the Candy King kept creeping closer and closer, even though I'd told him a few times I had a serious boyfriend. The flirtation had turned from flattering to bothersome to an SOS situation.

Come on Kat, I thought, *help a lady out.*

I'd spotted her a little while ago next to the bar, tilting her head to the side and cocking one hip down, which is a trick we both used to make our midsections look thinner. Then I'd looked away to deal with the hand on my leg and now she'd disappeared.

I could call a car service but I didn't have the phone number of one and, as I'd learned, no one at LA parties ever knew the number for a car, though from the look of how fast the liquor bottles were emptying, they really should've. But even if I'd had the number, I'd need to locate my phone first, which required me to locate my purse, which I'd abandoned somewhere in the vast, dim universe of the pool deck. It'd take forever to find it and in the process I'd almost definitely do something dangerous or humiliating, like step on someone's Manolo Blahniks or knock over an invaluable orchid. Kat could help me find it because Kat knew about my eyes—I'd told her back in college, before I'd taken a vow of silence about the subject. But in order for Kat to find my purse, I'd have to find Kat. Which brought me back to square one.

The thing to do, I concluded, was just stay put. Kat would come looking for me eventually, and since I was in public, I wasn't in any serious danger with the Candy King, though he had just taken the liberty of putting his arm around my waist.

"I really have to go," I protested, squirming away, but even as I said it, I knew he'd be thinking that if I *really* had to go, I would, simple as that.

He leaned over to whisper something in my ear, something about caramel. The whole thing had gotten real old, real fast. I wasn't laughing anymore.

"I'm sorry," I said, "I have a boyfriend."

"I don't mind," he replied.

I'll tell him I'm gay, I brainstormed, *though he probably won't mind that either. I'll tell him I have a VD. Herpes? No, syphilis. You can't argue with syphilis.*

Why confessing to fabricated syphilis was preferable than a retinal disease was beyond me. Mine was not to reason why. Mine was not to reason at all.

Just then, I felt a small, soft hand on my shoulder.

"What are you doing in there, crazy lady?" Kat was laughing behind me. "C'mon, I have your purse; let's get out of here."

"Thank God," I muttered, stepping out of the hot tub.

Within fifteen minutes, we were pulling up to the front door of my apartment building, with its Spanish-style roof tiles. Inside, I found David sitting on the couch, watching *The Twilight Zone* and eating pistachios.

"Why is your hair wet?" he asked.

"Why do you care?" I snarled back, storming into the bedroom. Because, of course, right along with the city of Los Angeles and Kat, David was fully to blame for the hot tub fiasco. If he'd come to the party, like I'd asked him, I wouldn't have ended up trapped in a hot tub with some lecherous moneybags; I would've had someone to talk to and a ready-when-you-are ride.

David was my default nighttime driver and it worked well enough when it was just the two of us going to dinner or a movie or visiting friends, something low-key that David liked to do. Whenever it was something he didn't like to do, there was usually a fight involved, or at least toxic levels of resentment on one side. Because there is a subtle but crucial difference between, "Hey, do you want to come to my agent's Christmas party?" and "Hey, do you want to come to my agent's Christmas party? And also, you don't have a choice."

In New York, David and I had had our own apartments, our own social circles; we were together sometimes but we were often apart. We acted as guardians of each other's solitude just like Rilke recommended. But as soon as we moved to LA, that changed. I no longer had the luxury of asking David to protect my solitude—he had to protect my nightlife instead. He still needed a solitude guardian but tough shit. I certainly wasn't going to start feeling sorry that he'd lost a bit of his freedom when I'd lost all of it. Who was the unfortunate one anyway?

Besides, it wasn't like I was inviting him to a root canal. This was exciting stuff; this was cocktails at the Standard, concerts at the Hollywood Bowl. Would it kill him to stop being such a homebody and start living his life, in the process making it possible for me to live mine, too?

"You know I hate this stuff," he said when I "invited" him to the birthday party of a USC director I'd recently struck up a friendship with.

"But you can pitch our movie to him," I told him, flatironing my hair in the bathroom. "I think Finn knows someone at Sundance."

"Don't pretend this is in my best interests," he replied. "If you need me to drive you, just ask me."

That knocked the wind out of me. I turned to him, wanting more than anything to press his balls between my flatiron. I hated him. And though I wasn't honest about my motives for inviting him places, I was honest about this.

"I hate you," I told him, turning back to the mirror. "I'd like to flatiron your stupid balls."

"Good," he said, "then you don't want me to come."

"No, I don't," I said, fingering gel through the ends of my hair to eliminate flyaways. "And I don't need you either."

"Just call a car," he suggested, turning on the TV.

"You know how much it'll cost to take a car to Silver Lake?" I shot back.

"What about Kat?"

"She's out of town."

"So, ask Finn to give you a ride," he said. "He won't mind."

"Just don't worry about it. I can take care of myself," I snapped, slipping on my Via Spiga sling backs.

"You still didn't tell him about your eyes, did you?" David said, looking at me over the tops of his glasses.

I ignored him. He just didn't get it. I was in the business of pretending to be better than I was. I'd just spent an hour making myself appear thinner, more buxom, and taller, with clearer skin, fuller hair and longer lashes. If I couldn't tell Finn, or any of the other acquaintances who were turning into friends, what my real weight was, I wasn't about to tell them I was half blind.

I dialed Finn's number anyway and asked if he'd give me a ride.

"My stupid car won't start," I explained.

"You need to bring that car in," he said. "It did the same thing last week."

"Yeah, it's a good-for-nothing piece of shit," I said, glaring at David. "You can't rely on it."

My dependence on David, which I refused to admit and he refused to ignore, was poisoning what was, in all other respects, a blossoming love. Needing someone to drive me places made me feel like a kid at best, a cripple at worst. It wasn't how I wanted to think of myself and it wasn't how I wanted him to think of me. Of course, as David tried to explain, that wasn't how he thought of me. Everyone needs help with some things, he said. And if I would only tell people about my limitations, they'd be glad to help, which would make him feel less hemmed-in and probably be a huge relief to me. It was easy for him to say. He could drive himself to In-N-Out whenever he felt like a burger.

But David wasn't opposed to my secret just because it inconvenienced him. He was disturbed by the way it was growing. What had started as a careful omission had become a bold, bald-faced lie. I made up stories to cover for bruises on my shin, knots on my forehead, mistakes I made when reading out loud. Put together, these little cover-ups created an alternate version of me, a version that kept getting boozier and ditzier to explain away the mistakes that were all attributable to my eyes.

David didn't particularly like this version of me and he got stuck spending a lot of time around her when we went out. He didn't understand why I'd prefer people to think I was obtuse and drunk rather than just partially sighted. I didn't understand it, or particularly like it, myself. But it was easier to keep going on the course I'd charted than start a new one.

Eventually, I reasoned, I'd tell people. When I had to. For the time being, I got by. Through a combination of feigning car problems, riding in Kat's passenger seat, and pushing David when I had no other options, I was able to avoid ever getting behind the wheel after dark.

But sometimes I'd already be behind the wheel as it grew dark.

Try as I might to ensure that whatever obligations I had would wrap up before dusk, sometimes things would run late and then I'd be stuck out after sunset. Sometimes I wouldn't notice; I'd be busy rehearsing and then suddenly look at the window and see the sun was almost set. Usually, I would notice but there was nothing I could do. I couldn't very well call, "That's a wrap!" midscene with a cast and crew on the clock because I was secretly night-blind.

Then, too, there was traffic. Sometimes I'd be stuck in gridlock on the 101 and watch, helpless, as the sky grew darker. My mind would scramble for a way out as my pulse rose and my palms started to get clammy. There was no way out. I was trapped behind the wheel, sinking in a sea of darkness.

One late afternoon, I was sitting in the waiting room of a casting agency in Sherman Oaks, waiting for my callback to play the wacky secretary in a new pilot. They were running late.

"Sorry," the casting assistant said. "We'll get you in really soon."

I nodded, swallowing. The sky out the window beside me was descending into a dusty gray and I had ten, maybe fifteen minutes left before twilight. I'd never been to this casting office before and I'd needed to consult my Thomas Guide the whole ride over. How would I see the Thomas Guide now? How would I see the street signs? How would I see the road on those curvy, tree-lined streets that took me over the hills? I tried not to sweat through my spearmint-colored shirt.

I'll worry about it after, I reasoned, *or else the whole callback is blown.*

As soon as the casting agent said, "We'll be in touch," I walked briskly out of the room, trying not to sprint in my knee-high boots. Once outside though, I did run, fumbling with my car keys and dropping them in my haste. The sky was darkening but mercifully, there were some weak rays of sunlight remaining. I could outrace the darkness.

Keys in ignition, foot on gas, buckling my seat belt as I turned the wheel.

Take it easy, I counseled myself. *Not too fast. Don't forget to look first.*

Once out of the parking lot, I craned my head forward, squinting at the street signs, trying to make out which one said "Deervale." A car behind me honked as I came to a near-stop at every intersection, trying to decipher the letters that were almost invisible.

"Hold your goddamned horses," I yelled, brave with my doors locked and windows up.

After passing through five intersections, I realized I'd gone too far. I would have to turn around. Five precious minutes had just leaked away and now the sky was dark purple, making it even harder to read the street signs.

Don't cry, I told myself. *No time.*

No matter how hard I strained, I couldn't make out the letters so I started counting letters instead of reading them. Four—no, that was too short. What was that? Six? No, "Deervale" was longer. This. Here. Eight letters. An "l" toward the end. This must be it. Yes. Go. Turn. Hurry.

The road was curvy but, thankfully, not crowded. I hunched over the wheel, gripping it with white knuckles. With the music off, I could hear the sound of my breathing, heavy, on the glass.

Just a little bit farther, I thought, *then I'll be on Ventura, which has plenty of light.*

I squinted my eyes and widened my eyes, experimenting, trying with sheer force of will to hold on to the shape of the cars in front of me, to keep the white lines that divided the lanes clear and distinct.

Just a little bit more.

My foot was heavy on the gas, pressing hard, urging the car forward, faster, faster, to make this miserable interlude end. I couldn't afford to look down at the speedometer but I knew I was going too fast. I could feel it.

Suddenly there was a flash of red in front of me, ripping me out of my trance. A car's brake lights, just ahead. I slammed on my own brakes hard, and closed my eyes, waiting for the impact. When there was none, I opened my eyes to see the car proceeding slowly through the intersection. I scanned the area until I located the reason the car had stopped. A stop sign. How many of those had I missed? How many more before I made it back?

There's no place like home, I thought. *There's no place like home.*

When I walked through the door of my apartment, I was shaking.

David stood up, alarmed.

"What happened?" he exclaimed, "Are you okay?"

I dropped my purse in our foyer and let my head and shoulders fall over like a marionette whose strings had been cut.

"Can we go home?" I said. "I want to go home."

PART II

Tip #10: On the sacrifices of pregnancy

When you become pregnant, your obstetrician will hand you a long list of seemingly harmless items that can kill or mangle your fetus. Monkfish? Beware. Hibiscus tea? Contraindicated! Peroxide? You want your kid to have arms or not?

Do whatever you want with this list. As long as you don't drink the baby's weight in grain alcohol and stop shooting heroin, I'm pretty sure it'll be okay.

There is, however, one item that should be on the list but won't be, since it doesn't pose a risk for most pregnant women.

I'm talking about heels.

Remember all those times you've found yourself facedown on asphalt because you missed a stair or got a heel caught in a crack in the sidewalk? Now think about hitting the pavement that hard with a baby inside of you.

Lose the heels.

Don't wean yourself off gradually; just gather all your darlings together, toss them in a garbage bag, and leave them at the doorstep of the Salvation Army like a Santa Claus for the frugal shoe addict. Then proceed directly to Target and buy yourself a bunch of sneakers. Practical, frumpy, I-haven't-had-an-orgasm-in-five-years-and-may-never-again, soccer-mom sneakers.

Yes, it's a sacrifice.

Better get used to those.

10. DAY OF THANKS

My father froze, the hypodermic needle poised in his hand.

"What?" he croaked.

"I don't have a parasite. I'm pregnant," I repeated. It wasn't how I'd planned on making the announcement, but desperate times call for desperate measures.

For once, there was silence at the dinner table. The floor-to-ceiling windows in my parents' apartment were open and I could hear the distant sound of cars honking twenty-four stories below. Ten pairs of eyes stared at me from around the table.

"What?" my mother asked, her voice low. She was holding a wooden spoon in midair, dripping marinara sauce onto the tablecloth. Only her eyes moved, and they were in full panic mode. "What?"

I thought perhaps they hadn't heard me right. This was the reaction I'd expect from "I'm moving to Canada!" or "I'm practicing Wicca!" or "I'm moving to Canada to practice Wicca!"

"You're gonna be a grandma," David elaborated. "Happy Mother's Day, everyone!"

Then my grandmother made a strange, gasping noise in her throat and began to sob, though it was anybody's guess whether they were tears of joy or anguish.

"*Mamma Mia!*" she choked out. "We gonna have a baby!"

When a twenty-seven-year-old, newly married woman begins vomiting incessantly for weeks on end, most people don't assume she contracted a parasite from her Hawaii honeymoon. Even if pregnancy doesn't pop up as the first explanation in most people's minds, chances are, it'd present itself as the second or third, certainly well before talk about running a CBC and differential, stat! Of course, my parents aren't most people.

To be fair, I did start the ball of paranoia rolling; instead of telling them I was pregnant at first, I told them I had the stomach flu. It was going around, I'd explained, making its way through the English program at Columbia, where I was weeks away from receiving my master's degree.

They bought this for a week or two, before they smartened up. This was no stomach bug.

"Listen, I don't want to alarm you," my father advised, "but you may have contracted *Helicobacter pylori*."

"I really don't think so," I countered.

"I'm sorry but did you get your medical degree when I wasn't looking?" my mother barked. "Your father is a PHYSICIAN!"

In the eyes of my family, my father's medical degree makes him an expert in everything, not just putting in a pacemaker, but assembling Ikea furniture and marinating chicken. He is the absolute best at doing absolutely everything. It's annoying, mostly because it's true. Drop the man on a desert island with a hanger and a pair of toenail clippers and he'd build an entire civilization, complete with high-speed Internet. Yet, despite his skill at nearly everything else, so far he was abysmal at detective work.

When I declined my father's invitation for a blood test, my grandmother became apoplectic.

"I beg you, *per favore*," Nonny pleaded, "Listen to you fadda! He knows what he's talkin' about!"

"For God's sake, look at you!" my mother went on. "You're wasting away!"

It was shocking, really, that women who'd experienced pregnancy firsthand would be incapable of recognizing its most common symptoms. If I let this go on much longer, they'd blame my third-trimester baby belly on too much Junior's cheesecake.

The rational thing would have been to just tell my family I was expecting. But I put off sharing the news with them, and it wasn't just because I was superstitious about going public before the twelve-week mark. I knew that once the announcement was made, it wouldn't be my baby anymore but ours. I knew they'd hijack my pregnancy.

When I was a teenager, in the face of my mother's dictums about what I could (not) wear and who I could (not) date, I'd yell, "It's my life!" and my mother would yell back, "It's your life I GAVE TO YOU!" Despite the fact that I hadn't been a child in a decade, my mother still acted like the deed to my life was in her name and I was just some renter she had to hand the keys over to who'd probably fuck the place up beyond repair. The woman still tried to order for me at restaurants, often implicating the waiter: "Oh, Nicole, don't get the chicken; you can eat chicken anytime. You always order the wrong thing! Excuse me, sir, but am I right? Isn't the veal better than the chicken?"

My mother wasn't the only controlling one; there was my grandmother and Aunt Rita to contend with, and to a lesser extent, my father, too. There'd been a thirty-minute debate the week before over what dress I should wear to my sister's rehearsal dinner, a debate that persisted despite me frequently yelling, "No one asked you!" and "You know I'm going to tell my therapist all about this tomorrow, right?" If they could be so overbearing about something so inconsequential, imagine the hell they'd raise when it came to child rearing. It's no wonder I kept the news of my pregnancy under wraps for as long as I could.

But during Mother's Day dinner in my eleventh week, when my father revealed the blood test collection kit, I realized the jig was up.

Within seconds, my grandmother was weeping, sporadically

invoking heavenly beings—"*O Dio!*" "*Madonna!*" "*Jesu mio!*"—and kissing the side of my face so that it was soaked with tears.

"You're happy?" I wanted to know. The intensity of feeling was clear, but what feeling it was, precisely, was harder to decipher.

"'Aaaaaaappy?" she wailed operatically. This is a woman who has perfected the art of talking while crying, probably because she spends so much of her time doing both. "A course I'm 'appy! And why not? I gonna have a baby!"

"*I'm* going to have a baby," I corrected her.

"Dat's what I said!" Nonny replied, patting my belly. "We gonna have a baby!"

My sisters and cousins abandoned their places at the table, swarming around me with questions.

Due date? Around Thanksgiving.

Baby's sex? Don't know yet.

Planned? Yes, thanks for asking.

What about a job, after graduation?

Writing articles for magazines. Freelance, to stay home with the baby.

Within a minute or two, my father was striding over, a crooked smile on his face, to shake David's hand and clutch me to his chest. My mother pulled me into an embarrassed embrace and joked about how no one had asked her permission before making her a grandma.

The mayhem had given them a chance to collect themselves, and the fanfare provided them with a cue. But I'd seen the panic in their eyes when I broke the news, and though they covered for it, the "What have you gotten yourself into?" expression was unmistakable as it passed across their faces.

I assumed the panic was related to the fact that the Blindness Deadline Dr. Hall had given me was just three years away, but I couldn't say for sure because they didn't verbalize their concerns. As always, we expertly maneuvered around the fat ass of the elephant in the room. I ignored the ambient tension and forgave the initial lack of enthusiasm. I could do this because, I, for one, was over-fucking-joyed.

I was concerned, of course, about my ability to take care of a newborn with my limited vision; and occasionally, in a quiet moment, the anxieties ambushed me. What if I tripped over a crack in the sidewalk while wearing the baby in the Mayan sling? I had already given up my heels—bequeathing them to my seventeen-year-old sister Jessica—but still, I could trip, could stumble, even without stilettos. What if I couldn't decipher the digital readout of the infant thermometer? What if I stepped on the baby by accident? This one worried me in particular because I'd done it once, when I was about eleven and Jessica was a year old. We'd been at Aunt Rita's apartment and since the crib had been occupied by my cousin, Jessica had been napping on a blanket on the dining-room floor. I'd run into the room with Marisa in hot pursuit and hadn't seen the baby there, slumbering on her stomach in what I now know was a mammoth blind spot in my lower peripheral vision. So I'd stepped on top of her, right on her little back.

"Ooooh!" nine-year-old Marisa gasped, "you squashed the baby!"

"Shut up!" I spat, watching the baby intently. How badly had I broken her?

I must've been light on my feet or maybe I landed more on her diapered butt than anywhere else but by some miracle, she hadn't been hurt. She'd just lifted her head off the blanket and looked around groggily for a second, as if trying to decide how pissed off to get. Then she concluded it wasn't worth the trouble, literally turned the other cheek to lay her head on the opposite side, and fell back asleep.

Now I was worried about repeating this mistake, and others far graver, with my own baby. But, I reasoned, I knew better than to put the baby to sleep on the floor.

There, I thought with relief, *one problem solved*.

I grew concerned, too, about pregnancy making my eyesight

worse. One night in my second trimester, I'd sat at my desk and summoned the courage to search the Internet for information on "mothers with retinitis pigmentosa." I was hoping that a similarly afflicted woman with kids would pop up in cyberspace and become my lifelong friend, mentor, and one-woman support group. What I found instead was a bunch of threads in which women with RP shared that pregnancy had seemed to accelerate their vision loss. It had never occurred to me that such a thing might be possible and now, way past the point of no return, was not an ideal time to find out.

I sat in the two-bedroom Park Slope rental we'd just moved into, surrounded by unopened boxes and unassembled baby furniture, and tried not to panic. Now that I thought about it, my vision did seem to be worse lately; there did appear to be new obstacles. It had become nearly impossible to read the *New Yorker* anymore unless I held it embarrassingly close to my face. I had stopped going to see foreign films because I couldn't make out subtitles unless they happened to be white letters against a black background. Tweezing my eyebrows had become a fool's errand.

Still, no dramatic change had occurred. And who really cared if I couldn't read the *New Yorker* anymore? I wouldn't have time to read once the baby was born, anyway. I focused my attention on getting ready for the baby—laundering onesies in chemical-free detergent, smoothing animal decals on the nursery wall, sterilizing pacifiers—and in doing so, managed to shake off the worry that pregnancy was shooting the fabric of vision full of bullet holes. No matter how little vision I ended up with, I would have plenty of love to give—a boundless abundance of love, I reasoned. And that would be enough, I was sure. Pretty sure. *Mezza mezz.*

Because I'd never really taken care of a baby before—little kids, sure, but never an infant—I was so clueless about what it entailed that my mind couldn't produce many specific concerns. Mine was just a vague glaze of anxiety, one that was easy enough to wash away with a flood of joy and excitement.

I remained elated through the months of morning sickness that had me yakking into grocery bags on the subway, through the ballooning of my belly like a mutant vegetable in a B movie, through the shooting nerve pain in my thigh that had me walking about as fast as a crippled tortoise, which was fine really, since that was the speed safest for my fetus, anyway. As my due date approached, I felt more and more excited, and when I woke on Thanksgiving morning to an unmistakable contraction, I was positively giddy.

And then the pain started, and the giddiness was obliterated.

It's not that the pain came as a surprise. Oh no: I'd been thoroughly prepared by my grandmother.

Nonny was the worst thing to ever happen to the natural childbirth movement. If home birth advocates knew she was running around sowing seeds of terror in the hearts of expectant mothers all across New York City, they'd have locked her up somewhere. With one sentence, she could crush nine months of hypnobirthing prep.

"*Dio mio,*" she moaned, transported back to the birth of her own daughters in the late 1940s, "I neva forget de pain! Madonna! De pain! I tought I was gonna DIE de pain was so terrible! Is someting you can neva imagine!"

I explained to her that nowadays the medical world has more to offer in the way of anesthesia than a leather strap and a shot of whiskey, but there was no interrupting the flashback once it began. She just had to let it run its course.

"De pain is so bad, you gonna beg to die. You understan' me? You gonna BEG—"

I stopped listening there. I'd get the epidural. She'd had me at "beg to die."

So when I went into labor, I expected the pain. I just didn't expect it to go on for so damn long.

I spent all of Thanksgiving day writhing around in my apartment before I decided I'd had it. It had been seven hours, which was a perfectly reasonable amount of time for a labor to last, and now enough was enough. No more screwing around.

In the eight minutes between contractions, I applied a full face of makeup using the magnifying mirror in my bathroom. Then I informed David: "It's time to go into the city. To the hospital."

"Did you just put on lipstick?" he asked. "And mascara?"

"What difference does *that* make?" I countered.

"I just don't know if it's time yet." He was ginger, not wanting to set me off. "Your contractions aren't close enough together."

It took every modicum of restraint not to crinkle up my nose and imitate what he'd just said in a nasal, singsong voice, like bullies do before beating the shit out of kids on the playground.

David is a by-the-book kind of person. If he's in the ten-items-or-less line at the supermarket and realizes that he has eleven items, he will get off the line, even if he is the next person to pay. He is the kind of person who makes an honor code actually work, the kind of person I refer to derisively as a goody-goody as I flash a student ID that hasn't been valid in years to get a discount at museums. In my defense, I'm an absolute straight shooter compared to my mother, who had my sisters and I ducking under the subway turnstile until we were in high school and has, on occasion, made a meal out of the free samples at Costco.

In general, I could appreciate that David's honesty was part of what made him a good match for me, the Jiminy Cricket to my Pinocchio. But in this particular instance, as it was standing in the way of me getting a hefty dose of morphine, I found it really fucking annoying.

"I don't care if they send me home," I said through gritted teeth, "I can't take it anymore."

Of course, David was right.

"You're not technically in labor," concluded my OB-GYN, Dr. Lamont, after examining me at the hospital. "You're no more dilated than you were at your last office visit."

"But that's impossible," I moaned. "It hurts. So much."

"Oh, it doesn't hurt yet," laughed Dr. Lamont, somewhat sadistically. "Your mascara is still perfect."

"How is that relevant?" I cried. "Why is everyone so fixated on the mascara? I want that epidural, just like you promised."

"Go home and eat some turkey." She smiled. "Well, maybe not the turkey. But a glass of wine, definitely. It'll help you relax."

Very much chagrined, I heaved my cervix out of that hospital that didn't want me. But the prospect of going all the way back to Brooklyn, walking up all those stairs, and continuing my writhing in our tiny apartment was unbearable. So I did something highly inadvisable.

I went to my parents' house. In the middle of labor.

Their apartment was in midtown, so in the event that I ever went into actual labor, I'd be close to the hospital. And besides, Thanksgiving dinner was just wrapping up. If we hurried, David pointed out, the meatballs would probably still be hot.

My grandmother greeted us at the door: *"Jesu mio!* De baby's coming! Did it start? De pain?"

She pulled me into the living room where my parents, sisters, aunt, and uncle were all scraping their plates clean and refilling glasses of wine while Pavarotti provided a little light night music. I felt like I'd been returned to the scene of my pregnancy announcement, only with a lot more physical agony.

My mother walked over.

"You don't look like you're in labor," she observed helpfully. "You're not even in pain."

"Oh, she gonna be," shuddered my grandmother.

A good-for-nothing contraction hit and I grabbed the edges of the glass dining-room table and closed my eyes.

"What's the matter with her?" Aunt Rita asked, with what sounded like a mouth full of meatball.

"She's having a *contraction,*" my mother called from the kitchen. "A little practice one."

"Well, we saved you some turkey," Aunt Rita announced, placing before me a heaping plate of turkey, stuffing, manicotti, meatballs, and fried cauliflower. Precisely the kind of light fare recommended in situations when you're about to push a human being out of your guts and are likely to shit yourself in the process.

"I can't eat," I panted, pushing the plate away. "The doctor said just some wine."

"*Vino?*" Nonny shrieked. "Wat kinda doctor is dis? A drunk? *Assolutamente no!*" She pushed the plate back toward me. "You gotta eat! You need you energy!"

"Don't you understand?" I pleaded. "I'm in pain."

"Well, I hope you're not planning to get an epidural," Aunt Rita pontificated. "Those drug your baby up and then they can't breastfeed and you'll have to use formula, which'll give the baby a lousy immune system and then you'll have real problems, I'm telling you."

Good God, I thought, *what have I done?* I was about to walk over to David and tell him discreetly to get me out of this madhouse when another contraction hit, and I had to drop onto my hands and knees. A captive audience.

"Since when you don't eat?" my grandmother shouted. "You gonna run out of energy right in da middle and den *finito!* De pain is gonna get you! You neva gonna make it!"

My mother drizzled sauce over the manicotti. "I hate to say it but she's right."

I shot David a desperate look but he was too busy gnawing on a drumstick to pay me any attention.

"Just let her see for herself," my aunt added. "She'll learn the hard way."

When the contraction eased up, I shoved a few forkfuls of manicotti in my mouth, just to shut them up for a minute. As soon as the next contraction passed, I told myself, we were going back to our place.

But in less time than it takes for a tryptophan coma to set in, something strange happened. I went from masticating manicotti against doctor's orders to floating buck naked in my parents' bathtub yelling, "Harder, harder!" as Marisa dug her fists into my lower back. Two hours had passed but I couldn't say how because the legendary pain had arrived. I was in a Manhattan high-rise but I might as well have been in rural Italy, begging the goatherd passing by to put me out of my misery.

My aunt and mother leaned against the bathroom wall, drinking red wine. My grandmother stood beside them, crying.

"I think you should try a different position," Aunt Rita suggested. "That's just my advice."

"What do we know, after all?" my mother joined in. "I've only had three kids—all natural childbirth."

I leaned over the edge of the tub and emptied the contents of my stomach onto the bathroom floor. This worked Nonny up to a frenzy: "Madonna! O Dio! De pain! De pain!"

I was ushered out of the tub and Marisa helped me get dressed, for which act of kindness I threw up on her. Before she'd had a chance to recover, I informed her that we had bigger problems.

"I think I peed my pants," I sobbed.

My sister pointed out that perhaps, seeing as I was in labor and all, my water had broken. I was so deranged by pain I'd almost forgotten that I was having a baby. I yelled for David.

"Hospital," I panted.

"You're still seven minutes apart."

I gave him a look that said, "I don't care how far apart the contractions are, if those doctors don't jam a needle full of drugs into my spinal column *like they mean it*, I will bitch-slap them with a bedpan." The great part about being married, even for only a year, is your spouse understands these looks without you having to say a word. Then I threw up on him, for good measure, and the matter was settled. To the hospital!

Dr. Lamont was impressed when she examined me. "You're at

seven centimeters. Good job! And your mascara is running all over the place! See?"

I was about to strangle her with my bare, suddenly crazy-strong hands, when she asked: "Want that epidural now?"

This seemed so absurd I began to cackle wildly. Did I *want* one? It was like saying, "Would you like me to untie this boulder from around your neck before I throw you in the river?" Yes, thanks, that'd be swell.

"Make it—a big one," I panted.

I couldn't make out the fine print on the paperwork the nurse brought over but it didn't matter. Even if it had said, "Epidural may cause the baby to come out of your mouth instead of your vagina," I think I would have signed on the dotted line.

Within a half hour, the magic drug cocktail was oozing into my system, bringing the giddiness back. I applied a fresh coat of lipstick so I'd look effortlessly beautiful in the postbirth pictures and then, before I knew it, Dr. Lamont was telling me it was time to push. She directed Marisa and David to each hold one of my legs, which made me feel a little like a wishbone. Things happened very quickly then and after a few pushes, the doctor said she could see the baby; it was that close.

After that, I didn't need any encouragement. I wanted to see that baby; I wanted to hold that baby; I wanted that baby here in the world with me—immediately. I pushed with an artery-popping force and within minutes the head crowned.

"Look down, Nicole," Dr. Lamont urged.

There was my baby, his face, his tiny, perfect face. I'd waited so long to see it and now here it was, and my God, it was beautiful. More than beautiful. It was sublime.

How can it be so tiny? I thought. *I never knew eyes and nose and mouth came in sizes this small.*

It was one of those moments where time freezes, a second that goes on and on and on, stretched like taffy and never breaking. I was mesmerized. I could not rip my eyes away.

I'm seeing this, I marveled. *Please let it last.*

Then I heard Dr. Lamont coach, "Come on, girl, one more push."

I bore down and watched as the baby's body—shoulders, arms, torso, and legs—poured out of me in an enormous rush. And as he slipped right out of my insides, into the world, I screamed.

Later, David would tell me it was the most animal-like noise he'd ever heard a human make and he thought I was tearing in two. But it wasn't pain. It was the sound of pure release; from my body was released another body, from my person, a person. My little person. Because, there in the doctor's hands, letting forth his own primal scream, was my Lorenzo.

David and my sister and I were all shaking and crying, in the moment now, the great moment that had broken open and was pouring over us. In the mix was joy and wonder and gratitude but holding it all together was this brand-new sensation, of grace, the kind of grace they always talked about in church, but I could never work my mind around.

"My baby, my baby," I kept repeating, "my baby."

I cried like it was me being born and in a way, of course, it was.

The doctor placed the baby, warm and wet, on my chest and as I watched he fluttered open the lids of his bee-stung eyes and reached for me, stretching his spindly fingers toward my lips. In that moment, it happened. I became a mother.

I know it was probably just coincidence that in his first earthly gesture, my son reached for me. I know he was really just writhing around in shock and disgust, madly attempting to scramble back into the womb. But it didn't feel like coincidence. It felt like a contract.

Will you have me? he was asking. *Can you?*

I will, I promised. *I can.*

In that moment, something changed in my anatomy, and I'm not referring to the fact that my stomach dropped back down from my chest to my abdomen, where it belonged. Suddenly, I had a new reason, a new purpose. From now on, what mattered most was caring for this tiny creature, making sure he was safe and happy. To do that, I would have to sacrifice. I'd sacrifice the things all parents do, like sleep and money and leisure. But I'd have to sacrifice something else, too, something that had become indispensable to me. I'd have to sacrifice the lie that I was like everyone else. I'd have to sacrifice the denial about my encroaching blindness, a denial I'd indulged in for more or less my entire adult life.

I looked at the naked infant in my arms.

For him, I'd do it.

Tip #11: On baby care

The good news is, you don't need to see to accomplish most of the big, important tasks of new motherhood. You can create a baby and deliver them into the world, with no vision at all.

The bad news is once you do that, you'll have a cantaloupe-sized human being with no abilities or defenses whatsoever who will be left in your care. The desire to keep this being alive will be roughly one billion times stronger than the most passionate desire you ever had before. And if you trip over a rattle on the floor, it could all be over. No pressure or anything.

The only answer is to go slow. Turn down your speed dial so that you're moving at half the speed you normally would, and then turn it down again, so that you feel like the room is filled with cannoli cream and you're just trying to wade through it. You'll know you're moving at the right speed if octogenarians pushing walkers are leaving you in the dust.

You still won't be able to prevent tiny and potentially fatal mistakes, but it's as much a guarantee as you, or anyone else really, gets.

11. BABY STEPS

When I imagined the halcyon days of new motherhood, I never imagined sobbing as I soaked my tits in a sitz bath in the toilet at 3:00 A.M. Yet there I was, wailing as loud as my newborn.

I'd known the first few weeks would be hard but this was like Armageddon. The effect of the baby's birth on my life was not unlike that of a demolition crew laying into me with a wrecking ball. Everything—my identity, my apartment, my lady parts—had exploded into chaos and now I was left to sift through the rubble to see what was salvageable and what needed to be replaced. Odds were good that the finished product would be an improvement over what was there before but that didn't mean the process wasn't ruthless.

In the first few weeks after Lorenzo's birth, unimaginably weird shit occurred on a daily basis. Usually, these developments were revolting and/or painful. Invariably, a medical professional assured me they were 100 percent normal.

Baby pissing directly into your eye during a diaper change?

Routine.

You passing blood clots the size of a fist?

Comes with the territory.

Scabs on your nipples?

Yeah, shit happens.

I'm no dummy but I did expect Life with Baby to more closely resemble a Pampers ad than, say, a carnival freak show.

What really troubled me was that I had no instinct anymore to sense what was okay and what wasn't. Not only were my nerves shot; my confidence was decimated.

The morning after Lorenzo was born, I was lying in my hospital bed, cradling the baby in my arms and gazing at his sleeping face, when he suddenly started to choke. On thin air. He hadn't been nursing or anything, he just went from slumbering in that unreachable, newborn way to gagging.

I lay immobilized for a second or two and then I raced into the hospital hallway, holding Lorenzo and yelling: "Help me! Someone! My baby is choking!"

I was fully aware of how ridiculous this sounded and what a spectacle I was making but my panic overrode any sense of decorum. This was life and death.

A middle-aged nurse strode over. She was built like a brick shithouse, solid in her scrubs, and she walked like she meant business. Within a few seconds, she'd grabbed the baby out of my arms like a sack of beans and whacked him on the back, twice, with what seemed like excessive force. I winced as I imagined his spinal column shattering. But he remained in one piece, as erect as a newborn can be, and his gagging was replaced with bawling.

"That's normal," the nurse explained, handing the baby back to me and paying precious little attention, I noted, to supporting his head. "He's just gagging on his amniotic fluid. They do that sometimes."

She said it casually, like it was supposed to make me feel better. In fact, it had the opposite effect. I'd been prepared to protect my son from all sorts of choking hazards—loose change, hot dogs, paper clips—but later, in a few months, when I'd had a chance to hone my mothering skills. I'd never thought I'd need to start now, right out of the gate, and that I'd have to also worry about him choking on stuff that was *already inside of him*. The very stuff that had shielded him from harm for the past nine months.

All of a sudden, the enormity of the enterprise before me slammed down on my shoulders. Holy Mother of God. There'd be things I would fail to protect him from. And not just the stuff I'd already, very diligently, worried about like clipping off his fingertips instead of his fingernails because I couldn't see details that small. There was a whole world, a whole galaxy, of other stuff that I couldn't protect him from, stuff that hadn't even occurred to me, stuff I didn't even *know* about. What the hell was I going to do now?

What I was going to do was hang my head and cry, which I did right there in the hospital hallway, in my no-slip socks and pink polka-dot pajamas.

"You mean he's going to do it again?" I sobbed. "And there's nothing I can do to stop it?"

Without missing a beat, the nurse put her hand on my shoulder and ushered me back to my bed. She seemed so unfazed by my sudden crying fit, it gave me the strong suspicion that that hallway had seen far worse mental breakdowns. Working in maternity was probably pretty similar to working in the psych ward, except with bigger maxi pads.

"It's going to be all right," she promised. "It's really harmless, you know. A little gagging won't hurt him."

"But what if—" I sputtered, "what if he chokes so much he can't breathe?"

"He won't," she replied. "I've never heard of that."

That wasn't sufficient reassurance for me. There was all sorts of shit you never heard about until it happened to you and then it was too late. I'd never heard about retinitis pigmentosa and yet, here I was, unable to see the tissue she was holding out to me until she finally shoved it right in my hand.

I blew my nose and took a deep breath. Too late to back out now.

"Tell me what to do, exactly, if it happens again," I pleaded. "Step by step."

"There's only one step," she replied. "Just give him a good old whack on his back."

"But how will I know for sure that his airway is clear?" I pressed.

The nurse looked over in the direction of my roommate who was buzzing her call button insistently from behind the room's dividing curtain. I'd been privy to my roommate's every sound for the last twelve hours and despite the fact that I hadn't caught a glimpse of her, I'd put together a pretty detailed profile: Polish, first baby, C-section, not much luck nursing, prone to sudden meltdowns herself. From the sound of the call button, there was another breakdown in the works, which meant mine had to be wrapped up.

"Look," said the nurse, "if the baby's crying, you know he's not choking. So I guess if you really wanted to be sure his airway was clear, make him cry. Give his big toe a good squeeze—that'll aggravate him."

"Okay," I affirmed, "got it." *If I have any suspicions that the baby is choking, any at all, I should make him cry.*

Which is why I spent the first month of my infant's life annoying him relentlessly.

I'd look over at the bouncy seat, where Lorenzo lay still, silent, and peaceful. Though this is most mothers' dream, it was my call-to-arms. Why was the baby so preternaturally still? Clearly, he was not breathing. Likely, it was that damn amniotic fluid causing trouble again. Who knew how long he'd been like this? As I sat pondering, his brain might be losing oxygen! No time to undertake the subtle investigative measures I'd learned in infant CPR class like watching his chest rise and fall; I couldn't trust myself to see the ever-so-slight movement of his chest anyway, my vision was so poor. No, no, this emergency called for the squeeze-the-toe test, approved by medical professionals as the quickest, most effective way to confirm baby's respiratory health.

I'd squeeze the toe. He'd scrunch his placid face into a scowl and commence caterwauling. Mission accomplished. The baby was breathing. And, now royally pissed off.

Over and over again in the first weeks of my baby's life, people were assuring me that if I trusted my mother's instinct, I'd be fine and over and over again, I was finding that was a load of horse crap. Maybe other mothers, ones with all their primary senses intact, had functional maternal instincts, but worry and a severe lack of confidence had caused mine to short-circuit. None of this mothering business was coming naturally. I needed a detailed instruction manual to do everything and sometimes, even that didn't work. Like with breastfeeding.

There are few areas in my life where I have ever been so bumbling. I was a hundred times more skilled at hammering nails into wood than I was at nursing and I had a 90 percent fail rate there. And—I hope he'll forgive me for saying so—Lorenzo was no ace himself. It was a classic case of the blind leading the blind. To make matters worse, there was nothing specific anyone could identify as the reason for why the whole thing was going so badly. I believe the clinical term for our situation was "cluster-fuck."

"Okay, let's get ready to nurse," directed the lactation consultant I hired for a house call on day four, after we took the baby for a weight check and discovered he'd lost too much weight. "Put your feet up. Adjust your pillow. Relax those shoulders. Now let's just try to get that baby's mouth wide open so he can get a good deep latch."

Already, with one hand holding my breast and one holding the baby's head, I was out of hands. But I stuck a finger out and attempted to gently caress the baby's cheek so as to trigger the whatever-the-hell-you-call-it reflex that was supposed to make the kid open his mouth.

I caressed and caressed, watching his mouth with so much intensity, sweat beaded on my upper lip. And then, finally, it happened—he opened, wide.

"Now!" yelled the lactation consultant. "Go! Go! Now!"

Placing her hands on top of mine, she grabbed the baby's tender little head, with all its terrifying soft spots, and slammed it onto my breast, like she was hitting the buzzer on *Jeopardy*.

Unfortunately, even the specialist lacked the lightning-fast reflexes necessary to attach the baby to my breast, because by the time the baby's mouth made contact, he'd already clamped his lips shut again. As much as this failed attempt frustrated me, it frustrated the baby a thousand times more. After all, he was the poor sap dependent on this whole thing for survival. He started bawling, that awful lamblike bray that makes nails on a chalkboard sound like Ein kleine Nachtmusik.

"Let's try again," the lactation consultant urged. "But wait—look at how hunched over you are. No good. And your hands—they're so tense! Relaaaaaaax. This is a perfectly natural experience."

So is getting lost in the woods and having a bear tear you limb from limb but I wasn't keen on doing that either.

I started to cry along with the baby.

"It's not working." I sniffed.

The lactation consultant placed her hand on my shoulder. "There's always formula," she offered.

I knew *that* before I shelled out $150 for a lactation consultant.

I was determined to nurse at all costs, not only because I'd read everywhere that Breast Is Best but because it was one mothering skill that had absolutely nothing to do with my eyes. There were so many other things I couldn't do as well as other mothers because of my failing vision, everything from safely walking down a flight of stairs to reading the dosage information on the gripe water bottle. But here was an ability I possessed that was in no way hindered by my vision, one area in which I could give my child the very best. Unfortunately, the very best came at a steep price.

Because I couldn't get the baby to feed correctly, I ended up with mastitis, a breast infection that treated me to a fever, flulike symptoms, and one rock-hard, flame red boob. This, in combination with waking every two hours throughout the night to feed the baby, as per my doctor's instructions, whipped me into a state of such severe fatigue I literally couldn't see straight. My already awful eyesight became even more hazy, my field of vision more constrained. Some people get fall-down drunk; I was fall-down tired.

One night, after I finally rocked the baby to sleep and laid him ever-so-gently into his bassinette, lifting one finger off his body at a time so as not to rouse him, I tiptoed over to my own bed a few steps away, and threw myself into it. Ever since I'd gotten pregnant, I'd forced myself to take extra care, and time, moving my body through space. Walking, like talking, was something I'd always done fast and I liked it that way, but I'd made the conscious decision to slow down, reminding myself that this excruciating, glacial pace was the velocity at which even nondisabled people moved outside of New York City. Still, I missed the luxury of physical abandon. So, once I'd deposited Lorenzo in his bassinette, I indulged in immoderation, letting myself drop like a stone onto the bed.

Except that there was no bed underneath me. I belly flopped, face-first, onto the hardwood floor approximately a foot to the side of the bed. The worst part was, the crash was so loud, it woke the baby.

David came running and found the baby and I crying in stereo.

"What the fuck?" was his well-formulated inquiry.

"The baby's fine," I sniffled, "But I'm all black and blue. I miscalculated."

"Nicole," he chastised, taking the baby. "You have to be more careful."

"How can I?" I wailed. "I'm a zombie. Like from your stupid movies." I liked the way that sounded so I repeated it as I sat on the edge of the bed and cried: "A zombie! A zoooooommmmmmbie!"

"Maybe you wouldn't be so tired if you didn't cry so damn much," David snapped, striding out of the room with the baby on his shoulder.

He had a point. Not that there was anything I could do about the incessant crying. The postpartum hormones were firing at me with both barrels and I was getting blown to bits.

I loved the baby so much it actually hurt—in my chest, a little like I was having a heart attack. In retrospect, it's possible I *was* having a heart attack, or at the very least a panic attack. Even so, there was no doubt that the force of my love for Lorenzo was unrelenting, consuming, brutal even. It was like when I pushed him out, I also pushed my heart out of my body and now I had to wear it on the outside without any protective barrier.

I found myself breaking down in tears on a daily basis, like I was training for the Crying Olympics. These sobbing episodes were unlike any I'd ever had. In my life before baby, I'd cried when I was sad, occasionally when I was angry. Now, I cried from a complicated combination of feelings whose primary ingredient was joy. I'd sit on the edge of my bed, staring at Lorenzo's tiny bowed lips, and then he'd flicker open his eyes and they were the very opposite of blind, they seemed to see things no human could ever see, staring off into space with such intense wonderment. Then his eyes would momentarily alight on me and I would feel an electric jolt, as if I were beholding something very pure and divine, not meant to be looked at directly. And I would weep with gratitude and joy, incredulous that he was mine.

And if you think that experience is fun, you're fucking nuts. There's a reason life pounds us into jaded, hardened assholes. David was right: that much feeling wears you out.

Of course, it wasn't all joy to the world and hosts of angels singing. Wrapped around the love, like a tumor on an essential organ, was fear. I was more scared than I'd ever been in my life. Hell, I was more terrified than the time I saw *Fatal Attraction* at a friend's house when I was twelve. I was shit-my-pants scared.

Because as I marveled at his perfection, I couldn't help but think, *I'm gonna fuck this up.*

There was no way I could take care of this baby. I wanted to, all right, and I'd give it my best shot but I was certain that I would screw up somehow and not just in a vague sense, like the kid would end up in therapy one day because I sleep trained him, but in a serious, awful way, like I'd trip on a diaper and crack his head open.

Lorenzo was so spectacular he deserved to have a professional take care of him. Whoever took care of the Princess of England's kids should be pushing him in his pram. Get the lady who wrote *What to Expect When You're Expecting* in here. Not me—shitty me, with my lousy eyes and my bleeding nipples. I wasn't good enough.

I wasn't just scared of how I'd fuck the baby up. I was also suddenly plagued by the fear that I'd be blindsided again with bad news, the way I was about my eyes, only about the baby this time. I couldn't stop worrying about how fickle Fate is, how you can be blithely buying bras one minute and hearing the words "incurable disease" the next.

The baby might be breathing fine now, but you never knew when SIDS might strike, silent and deadly in the night. You never knew whose friendly hand, shaking the baby's fingers, might be hosting a drug-resistant strand of *E. coli*. You never knew when a massive belch of amniotic fluid might resurface, obstructing the baby's tiny airway and causing brain damage.

In an effort to shield my baby from these misfortunes, I kept him inside, away from people except those I could nag into scrubbing well enough to enter an OR. I followed every guideline from the AAP. And I worried, incessantly, because you can't be blindsided if you're always prepared for the worst at every turn. Fate might do something awful to my beautiful baby but I'd be damned if I let her sneak up on me unawares again.

This worrying annoyed David because, as a new parent himself, he had no barometer by which to judge whether my reaction was rational and responsible or totally loco. We developed a detailed argument routine in seven parts.

1. I'd freak out about something small: "Do you hear that rattley sound? I think the baby has a snotty nose. Get the aspirator. Or should we look it up on the Internet first? Maybe we should page Dr. Frye. God, I hope this isn't early signs of RSV."

2. David would downplay the issue: "It's just snot."

3. I'd question his credentials: "How do *you* know?"

4. He'd insist I was being alarmist: "You don't have to be an expert to know kids get snotty noses. And you freak out about *everything!*"

5. I'd accuse him of shirking his responsibility: "You don't freak out enough! I have to do everything myself!"

6. He'd go for a low blow: "You're just like your mother."

7. And then, while I was taking a breath in order to verbally rip him a new asshole, he'd bring the conversation back to the baby: "If you're worried, just call Dr. Frye."

Which was always an excellent idea.

Dr. Frye had been highly recommended by my only friend with kids, Natalie.

"He's thorough and careful and great with the kids. And I trust his judgment completely," Natalie raved. "But I should say—he's not for everyone. He can be a little, ummm, opinionated."

"What do you mean?" I asked.

"It's just, he's not one of these low-key doctors who defers to you as the parent," she explained. "If he thinks you're doing something that's not in the kid's best interests, he's not afraid to tell you all about it. Like, he didn't like me using a crib tent with the baby, and he thought I should wait to pierce her ears. And he'll reprimand you if you let your kids watch too much TV. Stuff like that."

Sounded perfect to me: I intended to hold myself to the highest standards of mothering excellence and I was happy to find a pediatrician who'd help me do that. But by Lorenzo's first check-up it was clear that achieving mothering excellence was harder than I thought.

I was sitting next to David in a Sesame Street–themed examination room while week-old Lorenzo snoozed in David's arms and Dr. Frye took down our family's medical history. I was relieved Dr. Frye was asking the questions verbally; this way, he wouldn't catch me struggling to make out the print of a medical form.

"History of cancer?"

"No."

"Diabetes?"

"Yes, my grandparents had it."

"Blood disorders?"

"No."

"Any genetic conditions?"

I paused, blinking.

It was a standard question but, somehow, I wasn't prepared. It'd been eight years since my diagnosis and almost as long since I'd told anyone about my retinal disease, with just a few exceptions. I was embarrassed, uncomfortable. My mind thrashed around, trying to settle on a suitable answer. Did I have to tell him? I didn't tell other doctors I saw, like the gynecologist or podiatrist or anything. Maybe it wasn't relevant here either.

David looked at me expectantly. *Tell him.*

I glared back at him. *It has nothing to do with this.*

He raised his eyebrows. *If you don't, I will.*

Dr. Frye looked up from his chart.

"What is it?" he asked, scrutinizing me over the top of his eyeglasses. He looked suspicious.

"Oh, nothing, it's just . . . I, um, I'm not even sure this is relevant," I stammered.

Why was it so hard to share this straightforward piece of medical information with a doctor? If there was ever a place where it should be easy to tell someone about my eye disease, this was it, yet every last atom in me strained to keep the information concealed. I felt like uttering the diagnosis would make it airborne, contagious, and I didn't want that disease mentioned, even tangentially, in relation to my baby.

Then, too, I was vain. I didn't want this doctor, who I was trying to impress with my impeccable parenting, to know about my big, irremediable flaw. What if he judged my decision to become a mother? Couldn't I wait until he got to know me better before I told him?

"Well?" Dr. Frye pressed. "Are there any genetic conditions or not?"

"Ummmm, sort of," I mumbled.

"I'm confused," replied Dr. Frye. "This is a simple question."

"She has a retinal disease," David piped up. "It's genetic but no one else in the family has it, so the specialist we saw said our kids would have about the same chance of having it as anyone else's kids, in the general population."

"What's it called?" Dr. Frye asked, and I told him, along with all the other pertinent details. He didn't look disappointed in me or sorry for me or even that interested, which made sense, of course, because the guy hardly knew me. The whole thing took about two minutes and then it was in the chart and it was done.

On the walk home afterward, I flagellated myself. The doctor needed to know our medical background to keep Lorenzo healthy. Didn't I want my son healthy? What the hell was I doing, putting vanity and fear before Lorenzo's well-being? Hadn't I just vowed, when he was born, to sacrifice everything for him?

My eye disease didn't belong just to me anymore; it was part of his story, too, and I no longer had the luxury of keeping it confidential. To take good care of him, I'd need to be honest about my limitations so I could enlist the help of other people, to measure out the Infant's Tylenol, to locate him when he started walking, to check his head for lice when there was an outbreak at school. I had a long road ahead of me and I could not go it alone.

I knew I'd have to come clean with my secret.

I just didn't know it would be so hard.

Tip #12: On stepping in it

Prepare to step in a lot of shit. I am speaking literally here. The world is full of canine excrement and when you can't see out of the corner of your eye, there's no way to maneuver around it. This is an unpleasant fact of blind life.

Walking in dogshit, however, will seem positively delightful after you've slipped on the carcass of a dead animal. Like uncollected dog turds, sidewalks accumulate a rather revolting amount of roadkill—rats, squirrels, pigeons—and unless you shuffle around with your eyes glued to the pavement like a little old lady, eventually you're going to place your foot right inside some slimy, flattened pigeon intestines.

I have no advice to prevent this; I'm just giving you a heads-up so you can get yourself used to the idea. I do suggest, though, that you avoid sinking too much money into footwear, so that when it does happen and you're hopping around the street shrieking, "HOLY MOTHER OF GOD, MY FEET ARE FUCKING COVERED IN RAT GUTS!" you won't feel guilty about tossing those shoes into the nearest trash can.

12. THE MOTHERLAND

There's nothing like seeing a man cemented in volcanic ash to make you appreciate life.

"Holy crap," I marveled, turning to David. "Is this, you know, appropriate for the baby?"

"He doesn't know what he's seeing," David reassured me. "Besides, this isn't a horror movie. It's history. The kid's seeing Pompeii and he's not even two years old yet."

"You're right," I agreed.

I stood there next to David and Lorenzo in his stroller, looking at the petrified corpse and feeling incredibly good about myself.

We are a great family, I thought, *and I am a stellar mother.*

My self-congratulation was pierced by a wail so thunderous it threatened to crumble the ruins.

"Baaaaaaaaa-BUUUUUUULLLLL!" shrieked one-and-a-half-year-old Lorenzo, a sweating, writhing mass of limbs in his Maclaren Volo.

"Where's his bottle?" I asked David, translating from Lorenzese.

"We ran out, remember?" He produced the empty bottle, an Italian *biberone* we'd bought a few days ago after Lorenzo had thrown his last American bottle over the railing in the Coliseum. He'd sucked down the last dregs of milk a few hours ago on the train from Rome and I'd made a mental note to fill 'er up, but as we weren't traveling with our own cow (I had ceased being one a few months before), this was hard to accomplish.

"Oh shit," I said, biting my lip. "Now what?"

The baby needed his bottle. If that plastic nipple was not shoved in his mouth in the next minute or two, sending gulps of creamy goodness down his gullet, we were going to have a situation. Imagine being stranded on an island with a toothless meth addict who'd just smoked the last of his stash and you will get a sense of the panic and foreboding we felt then.

"Let's get out of here," I instructed, grabbing the stroller handles. "Before he blows."

Before we'd come to Italy on our first family vacation, David and I had been in the process of weaning Lorenzo off the bottle, as per the recommendation of Dr. Frye. We had a very complicated weaning schedule, which involved him reducing the quantity of milk he consumed as well as the frequency with which he consumed it. I'd spent weeks chastising my grandmother, who babysat Lorenzo, for caving and giving him the bottle before the appointed Bottle Time.

"Eh-oh, Mussolini! Wat's a matter wit you?" Nonny rebuked me. "You making dis poor baby suffer! He's a baby! He needs his baabull!"

Of course now we were in Rome, doing as the Romans did, and that meant letting the kid drink as many bottles as he wanted. By Italian standards, he had another two, three years before we even needed to think about cutting him off. Ditto on diapers, and the paci.

"Wow," remarked David one night as we passed a boy in Piazza di Spagna cursing in Italian at his video game while sucking on his binky. "I don't think they'd blink if I started using a paci again."

"Yeah, it's no coincidence they use the word *bambino* to refer to kids until they're teenagers," I said. "Here, you're a baby until you turn into a man."

I thought of my old Venetian beau, Benedetto, who'd be nearly forty now and probably still living with his mamma: "And then, in some cases, even after, too."

It hadn't taken long, though, for our derision for Italian-style parenting to morph into jealousy. Sure, these kids stayed in diapers till they were almost old enough to say, "Mamma, I shit-a my pants!" but so what? Why the big rush to grow up, anyway? You were only a baby once, after all. And besides, it would make life a helluva lot more enjoyable not to be so exacting all the time. So, even though I knew Dr. Frye would pop an artery about it later on, we scrapped bottle weaning, and bedtime, too. Before you knew it, Lorenzo was chain-drinking milk out of Big-Gulp-sized bottles and staying up until midnight, after which point he'd climb into bed right between David and me.

It felt fantastic to loosen up our terribly American rigidity—and between the laissez-faire parenting, the siestas, and the red wine at every meal, David and I were having one hell of a vacation. It was like a second honeymoon, only with a lot more scrubbing urine out of bedclothes.

We needed it, too. The first few months of Lorenzo's life had been hard on our marriage. It wasn't just that Lorenzo woke us every two hours all night long like he was a Navy Seals drill sergeant until we cowered under the covers in fear, unable to sleep even when he was quiet. It wasn't just that David had watched my body, previously an object of desire, transform into something that belonged in a medical encyclopedia. More troubling than all of this was the fact that David had been instantly demoted from the love of my life to the man who changed the diapers of the love of my life. David couldn't help but feel like a third wheel as I nuzzled the baby and laughed at the baby and hung on the baby's every gurgle as if he were Confucius. But by the time Lorenzo was about six months old, my body had recovered, his sleep had stabilized, and my hormonal monomania for the baby let up a bit, which allowed David and I to find our way back together again. And by the time Lorenzo started walking and talking, David had fallen in love with him, too.

David could do stuff with Lorenzo now. He could read him his childhood copy of *Where the Wild Things Are*. Lorenzo danced along when David played Dylan and the Drive-By Truckers. The two of them could even have a conversation, albeit pretty one-sided, about the superiority of Marvel over DC comics. Whereas Lorenzo and I enjoyed a Vulcanesque mind-meld from the very start, it took David some time before he'd bonded; but now they were tight.

It helped that Lorenzo looked just like David, with thin tufts of pale yellow hair and eyes the color of a swimming pool, a deep cyan. His eyes were so startlingly lovely—big and wide and blue like the sky, "celestial" my grandmother called them—that Italians would stop us to take pictures on their cell phones.

It was a regular lovefest in our family, one that was only heightened by our transatlantic trip. Although now that we'd run out of milk in Pompeii, things were taking a definite turn for the worse.

"BAAAAAAAA," bellowed Lorenzo so ferociously he was forced to pause and take another breath to finish the word, "BUUUUUULLLLL." His face said, "Did I stutter? *What* is the holdup here?"

I tried to hand him his lovey—a stuffed monkey named Earl—but ended up tripping over the cobblestones and tossing Earl into an ashy dirt heap, which might have been human remains. Those damn cobblestones were beautiful and all but not a friend of the tunnel-sighted. Which was unfortunate for me, since they were everywhere.

"Let's just head to the nearest bar," I yelled over Lorenzo's shrieks, dusting Earl off, "by the train station. We'll buy him a glass of milk."

"Lead the way," David agreed.

"Me?" I protested. "*You* lead the way."

A half hour later, we were standing on a hillside covered in white flowers, watching a sheep amble by. We were approximately a hundred miles away from a bar, or any other evidence of civilization.

"David," I ventured cautiously, "can we agree now that we are—"

"We are not lost," he barked, turning the stroller in the direction of a dirt road. "I am sure we can get out this way."

"Baabull?" Lorenzo whispered weakly, looking up at me with hopeful eyes. "Baabull, Mama?"

"You should have let me ask someone where the exit was when there was still someone to ask!" I snapped.

"You should have read the signs!" he snapped back.

"*You* should have read them!" I shrieked. "I can't see the print."

"Well I can't read ITALIAN!"

"Who the hell's going to help us now?" I whined. "The sheep?"

"Baabullbaabullbaabullbaabullbaabull," moaned Lorenzo, in a real delirium now. He looked like a man in the throes of the Spanish flu, shaking and rolling his head from side to side. "Baabullbaabull-baabullbaabull."

"I am beginning to wish I was one of those guys encased in lava," David said.

At that moment, an explosive sound echoed out of the stroller. It was the unmistakable sound of a child shitting himself in his very last diaper.

I gasped. "No. Fucking. Way."

After a pause, the thunderous sound commenced again. And again. And again. Lorenzo was taking a dump as epic as ancient Rome itself. We were up shit's creek without a diaper.

"Well, here we are. It's us. We are the ruins of Pompeii," David observed.

"*AIUTO!*" I bellowed in no particular direction, "Help!"

It only took five more minutes of screaming before a grounds-keeper who looked to be about 110 hobbled over. He was very kind and insisted on escorting us to the road that led to the train station, although to describe the speed with which we walked to be a snail's pace would be insulting to snails. An hour later, we reached the train station where we purchased a glass of milk for Lorenzo and a stiff drink for David and me. The bar didn't carry diapers so we were forced to bring shit-encrusted Lorenzo on the train, and though we were humiliated by the grimaces of the other passengers, it ended up working in our favor. Turns out a kid who's crapped himself is better than an unwashed homeless person to clear out a train car. There's always a silver lining.

The next day we boarded the train again, only this one was headed to the beach. We were traveling to Terracina, a coastal town about an hour south of Rome, where my mother and aunt Rita used to spend summers as kids. We'd be staying at my aunt Rita's apartment, just in time for Ferragosto.

Ferragosto is a fascinating Italian holiday for which there is no American equivalent. The date, August 15, commemorates the Assumption, which is when the Virgin Mary ascended into heaven. That, in and of itself, is cool. Mary deserves her own holiday, if only for not freaking out about the whole immaculate conception situation. Over time, though, the celebration, which you'd think wouldn't get wilder than a bunch of lit candles and an all-Latin mass, has become a balls-to-the-wall blowout beach rager complete with skinny dips and widespread public intoxication. The Virgin Mary must have more fans than one would think. That, or August in Italy is party month and an Assumption is as good a reason as any, and better than most, to party hard.

Starting the first week in August, Italian businesses in the big cities hang signs in their windows that read CLOSED FOR FERIE as inhabitants head to nearby beaches or mountain towns for the rest of the month. No one anywhere feels like working in August and in Italy, the cityfolk basically just agreed that they wouldn't. Some Flavia or Fabio one day just said, "Oh, to hell with this daily grind. I'm fucking doing it; I'm taking the whole month off," and then everyone started doing it and now if you find yourself in Rome anytime in August, your choices for dining out are McDonald's or Burger King.

By Ferragosto Eve, August 14, sleepy beach towns like Terracina are bulging with tourists who have perfected the art of partying over the past two weeks and are looking for a climactic night to take their revelry to the next level. The midnight ocean swim and subsequent all-night beach party is on par with New Year's at Times Square, only with a lot less clothes and a lot more cigarette smoke.

What made the celebration especially exciting for us is that Ferragosto Eve happened to be David's birthday. We told Lorenzo that Italy was going to throw Daddy a huge birthday party with fireworks and music, where everyone in the whole town would go swimming in the ocean at nighttime. It would be, I promised, the crown jewel of our Roman holiday.

Of course when the big night came, we were too tired to go.

David and I were, that is. Lorenzo was all revved up, running around the apartment buck naked at 11:00 P.M.

"Well, should we rally?" I asked David, turning my head on the pillow to face him. After a day of chasing Lorenzo on the train and in the beach and out of the street, David and I looked like we'd taken one too many horse tranquilizers.

"Do you want to?" he muttered, hardly moving his lips. He was lying beside me on top of the sheets, eyes shut.

"Do *you* want to?" I mumbled back.

"Uh-huhhhhh," was the sound from David's mouth. It was more of a snore than a reply.

"Yeah," I agreed, rolling onto my stomach. The road to the beach was so dark and uneven, I hated having to brave it after sundown. The night before, we'd gone into town to get a gelato and I'd stepped directly into the slimy guts of a run-over pigeon, which were so slippery, I'd thought for a minute I'd stepped on a banana peel. I'd been wearing flip-flops and had to scrub my foot for a half hour before I felt clean, like a less poetic, more gross version of Lady Macbeth. Who wanted to repeat that? Better to skip the party this time.

"YAAAAAAAA!" came a screech from the living room. It grew louder and louder until Lorenzo was shouting directly in my ear. He pounded my back and chanted cheerfully: "WAWA! WAWA! WAWA!"

"*He* wants to go," I told David.

Lorenzo shimmied off the bed and began yanking on our feet, attempting to drag us out. By way of explanation he offered: "Wawawawawawawawawawa!"

"You sure??" David asked Lorenzo, his arms still folded in corpse pose.

"Ya! Ya! Ya!" chanted the baby. I lifted my head to look at him and the thrill of getting eye contact set him a-chortling, his mouth gaping open so much it made the skin on the top of his nose crinkle and his tiny teeth show.

"Okay," David said, sitting up slowly, "Let's do it."

An hour later, we were standing in the sand staring at the dark waters of the Mediterranean Sea. Us and every other person with a pulse in Terracina, including a few very wrinkled old ladies whose pulses were pretty borderline. Techno music blared from the beach-front dance clubs and DJs were shouting into their mikes, pumping the crowd up for the countdown to midnight. Lanterns had been strung up along the boardwalk but it was still too dark for me to make out much of anything. I did discern a little boy in a Speedo drop trou and piss into the sand directly in front of us. Somewhere to my left, I heard clinking bottles and a bunch of teenagers cursing each other's mothers.

Lorenzo danced around the beach in his diaper, stomping on the sand and chanting, "Wawa! Wawa!"

"Not yet, honey," I told him, reasserting my grip on his arm to ensure he didn't dart out of my sightline. "We have to wait til they yell, '*UNO!*'"

"C'mere." David lifted Lorenzo into his arms. "Daddy will carry you in."

The shape of the two of them was just barely discernable by the lantern light, more unseen than seen. But for me, the fact that I could make out the shine of Lorenzo's eyes at all was a victory.

I'm making it work, I thought to myself. Then Lorenzo squealed and pointed to the ocean where someone had released a fleet of paper boats carrying candles and I amended the thought.

Fuck that, I thought, *I'm kicking ass and taking names.*

When he was a baby, I'd been concerned that Lorenzo would miss out on things, that my handicap would limit his life experience. But in the past two weeks Lorenzo had lit candles at St. Peter's, tossed a coin in the Trevi Fountain, seen (and become) the ruins of Pompeii. And now my son was about to swim in the Aegean Sea at midnight. The kid wasn't missing out on much.

Lorenzo wasn't the only lucky one. I'd been fortunate enough to see all of it, every milestone, from his first bites of food (carrots), to his first steps (Halloween night) to his first scrape (elbow). I wasn't missing out on anything either. My eyesight was mercifully holding steady, making me not only enjoy motherhood tremendously, but feel good at it, too.

Boosting my confidence was the fact that I'd weathered the transition of Lorenzo becoming mobile. I'd been terrified of the kid learning to walk, and run, and climb, and now he was doing all of those things but somehow both of us were not just surviving, but thriving. Enough that I'd decided to stay in Italy with Lorenzo for another two weeks after David went back to work in New York.

Sure, the kid narrowly avoided getting plowed down by Vespas on a daily basis, but that could happen to anyone, and besides, he hadn't actually been hit. I'd managed to rescue him just in the nick of time, even with no peripheral vision.

It wasn't so hard really; all it required was that I never take my eyes off him unless he was physically attached to me, and that I run on hyper-drive, at Maximum Level Alert every waking second. Yes, it was exhausting, but that's why God invented espresso.

I'd been managing so well, in fact, that I hadn't even needed to start telling people about my vision loss. When Lorenzo was a newborn, I'd readied myself to bite the bullet, but then I'd discovered I didn't need to really, that I could handle this parenting thing on my own. David lent me his eyeballs for the detail work, and that filled in the gaps, for now. Eventually, of course, my vision would get so blurry and constricted that I'd have to reveal my limitations to the world, but I'd cross that bridge (or jump off) when I came to it.

"DADA!" Lorenzo screamed, slapping his little hands on David's left pec. A new tattoo stained the skin there, a few inches from the place where my name was marked on his arm. Etched in red and blue ink was a human heart, with four chambers and ventricles, and underneath in capital letters was Lorenzo's name. David had come home with it a few days after the baby's first birthday and Lorenzo was fascinated by the image, even if he didn't understand what it meant.

"Oh, here they go," David told Lorenzo. "Get ready."

"*Nove, otto, sette,*" chanted the crowd, along with the DJ's booming voice.

"David," I said, feeling down his arm until I found his hand and slipping mine inside. "Don't let go."

I needed to hold his hand but I wanted to, too. We were taking the plunge together.

"*Sei! Cinque! Quattro!*"

"YA! YA! YA!" Lorenzo chanted along with the crowd.

"*Tre! Due!*"

David tightened his hand around mine and then, "*UNO!*" boomed the crowd. Just as if an invisible gate had been raised, the people on all sides, the men and women and children, poured into the ocean. David pulled on my hand and we ran together, Lorenzo bouncing in his arm. I couldn't see anything for a minute, only perceived the darkness deepening as I turned my back to the boardwalk lanterns. Then, suddenly, my feet met water and my front was splashed with cold. I let go of David's hand and holding my breath, dropped down into the quiet below the surface.

When I popped back up, gasping and sputtering, the sky wasn't black anymore but red and orange and white. Cracks like thunder exploded overhead and for a second, I cowered, unsure what was happening, Then I saw the colors falling in pieces out of the sky and a new burst of color radiating out from an epicenter that seemed to be directly over my head. Fireworks.

There was a splash beside me. I felt David's hand in mine again and I heard Lorenzo shriek an unintelligible squawk, equal parts terror and wonder and jubilation. It was a perfect expression of the feeling in my heart.

"See the colors?" I said. "See all the pretty colors."

We watched the fireworks bloom, big enough for even me to see. The whole scene was electric and I felt totally plugged in, as ablaze as the pyrotechnics overhead.

The fireworks lit the water so bright that I could see Lorenzo's face clearly, his eyes a wide, unblinking blue. He was mesmerized.

Thank you, I prayed, *for letting me see this. For letting me see him see this.*

"I can't believe we almost missed it," I whispered to David.

"I know," came his voice next to me.

Were it not for Lorenzo, I thought, *we'd be snoring right now, having traded in a once-in-a-lifetime experience for an hour's more sleep.* Though we'd traveled four thousand miles for this midnight swim, we almost didn't make it the very last quarter of a mile. But the littlest of our clan had rescued the night, and now none of us would ever forget it.

Later that night, once Lorenzo had finally surrendered to sleep, David and I curled up together. We'd gotten our second wind all right, and were still feeling pretty electric. This, combined with the fact that David would be leaving for New York the day after next, whipped us into an amorous mood. Whipped me at least. David is always prewhipped, at the ready should we ever find ourselves alone with ten minutes to spare.

In the middle of our carnal embrace, David paused for a prophylactic and I stopped him.

"Don't use one," I whispered.

This was not something we'd planned. I mean, we'd discussed that we wanted another baby eventually, but not necessarily nine months from now. Unlike other women, though, who approach the decision to have another baby with timetables, ovulation charts, and lists of pros and cons, I had exactly two points to consider: 1. I loved being a mother and 2. I wasn't blind yet. The longer I waited, the more my retinas would deteriorate; the more they deteriorated, the harder parenting would be and the higher the probability that I'd make some colossal mistake that would make it impossible for me to justify having another child. Not just to David, who trusted me and followed my lead, but to myself.

The window of possibility was still open but inching closed all the time. So I asked David to take another leap of faith.

"Are you sure?" David asked.

"Yes," I replied, breathless, "yes yes yes."

Tip #13: On telling your child about your vision loss

I suggest tackling this conversation while your child is still young, so young, in fact, that he may not even remember it, and certainly won't have the vocabulary to tell anyone about it. Kids can't keep a secret for shit—unless they lack all verbal ability.

13. PLANNING PARENTHOOD

"No! No! No!" Lorenzo yelled, squeezing my lips together with his chubby fingers.

I pried his fingers off my face, carried him swiftly into the living room, and plopped him in front of his box of toys. Of course, neither hell nor high water—and certainly not a bunch of wooden trains—would keep him there; when I raced back to the bathroom, he was right behind me. Then I had no choice but to fend him off with the back of my arm, like a nightclub bouncer controlling the crowd; I didn't want to blow chunks directly onto the child.

"'TOP, MAMA!!!" Lorenzo shrieked, redoubling his efforts to prevent me from vomiting. I'd have loved to hear why, exactly, he was waging a one-man battle against my morning sickness, but since he wasn't even two years old, he couldn't offer much in the way of clarification. He was like a well-intentioned but deranged vigilante; he'd protect me from my own vomit, no matter how much I begged him not to.

I gritted my teeth tight, feeling like the First Chinese Brother That Swallowed the Sea. With one hand, I fended Lorenzo off and with the other, I wrestled with the toilet lock we'd put on to keep the kid from playing with his bath toys in the shitter. Highly effective, that thing. Too effective, really.

"MAMAMAMAMAMAMAMAMA!" Lorenzo screamed, frantic now. Great. Now in a minute, on top of everything, I'd have my neighbor knocking on the door, asking if everything was okay in here.

Just as I was reaching the absolute limit of my ability to hold back my puke, the toilet lock popped open, and I took careful aim, honed through weeks of practice. In under two minutes, I was washing my mouth out at the sink.

Lorenzo crumpled into a defeated heap and sobbed. He'd lost the battle again. I felt genuinely sorry for the kid.

"Oh, honey," I murmured as I sank down to the floor beside him, "I'm so sorry. Mommy can't stop it. But it's okay. It doesn't hurt. I'm just working hard to grow a baby in my belly."

I was only a few weeks into my second pregnancy but already, it was shaping up to be harder than I expected.

I'd had terrible morning sickness with Lorenzo, the kind that makes other women hateful because I had to intentionally *try* and put weight on during my pregnancy. I found this to be compelling evidence that the only diet that gets fast, dramatic results is bulimia. Not that I'd recommend it; I'd far rather be full-figured than walk around puking in my hand. I tried every home remedy out there—peppermint gum, saltines, B6, ginger candies from Chinatown—and all they did was change the taste in my mouth when I threw it all up again. I tried acupuncture and sea bands and sniffing handkerchiefs doused in lemon verbena oil like a Victorian gentlewoman but I just kept on tossing my cookies until I delivered Lorenzo, at which point I immediately felt better.

The memory of this nausea marathon was very clear in my mind when I got pregnant with Number Two, but I was convinced that this time would be different. This time, I'd be that beatific, glowing mother-to-be doing downward facing dog and drinking smoothies.

Of course, the only downward-facing position I ended up in was with my head over a toilet.

In fact, when I looked back, I couldn't recall what could've been so bad about upchucking a few times a day, when I was free to do so without a tiny madman hell-bent on stopping me.

The vomiting wasn't just miserable in and of itself; it also served as a reminder that my body was under a lot of strain, and this made me worry about my vision. During my first pregnancy, I'd noticed my eyesight worsen—at least I thought I did. It was tough to tell since the change was vague and hard to quantify. It was now a challenge to read the price slapped on items at the grocery store. The glare on sunny days was as blinding to me now as nighttime, and I couldn't leave the house without sunglasses. Navigating stairs in dimly lit brownstones required me to use my foot almost like a cane, tapping my heel on the back of each step to judge its depth and width. When I was writing articles on my laptop, I kept having to enlarge the font size, first to 14, then 16, then, begrudgingly, 18.

What all of this boiled down to was: my vision had gotten worse since I'd gotten pregnant the first time. Now that I was pregnant again, who knew how much worse things would get?

When I brought it up to my latest retinal specialist, a perfectly unobjectionable but rather noncommittal doctor, he said he'd heard a similar complaint from other mothers with RP, though there was no hard and fast proof that pregnancy accelerated the disease's progress.

All I knew was that I looked like a woman being eaten away by a deadly parasite—wan, gaunt, prone to fainting—and it stood to reason I'd lose a few more rods and cones than when I was well. All I could do was hope it wouldn't be more than a few. In any event, it was a small price to pay for what I'd get in return. And besides, it did no good to worry.

This, however, was a perspective I knew my parents and

grandmother would not share; they were wired to worry, whether it did any good or not. So I decided not to tell them about the pregnancy for a while, though this was easier said than done. After all, David, Lorenzo, and I ate dinner at my grandmother's house in Bensonhurst on a regular basis.

Nonny, ever-attuned to what went onto her guests' plates, couldn't help but notice that I wasn't eating much; all I had on my plate was a slice of Italian bread and a few pieces of penne with the sauce pushed over to the side. This, of course, aroused her suspicion.

"Wat's a matta wit you?" she asked, eyeing me skeptically from the stove, where she was frying up riceballs. "You not eatin' anything!"

"I'm eating," I protested.

"Wat happen—you don't like da bolognese sauce?" she persisted, "I woke up at four o'clock dis mornin' to make da sauce."

"No, no, I like it," I assured her, "it's just—I'm—I'm on a diet."

The famously effective bread-and-pasta diet.

"Ohhhhh," she murmured, nodding her head, "Dat's good. You hadda beautiful figure before you hadda Lorenzo."

"Thanks, Nonny," I replied, glaring at her. "Thanks a lot."

"You know wat? It's workin'," she observed. "You lost alotta weight."

I figured this would satisfy her for a few weeks. It satisfied her for exactly thirty seconds.

"But now dat's enough, don't go overboard!" she ordered, placing a cutting board piled with sliced salami in front of me. "Eat some a dis soppressata I got for you. Maria's cousin brought it from Sicily, in her suitcase."

The thought of ingesting any kind of meat product, much less one that had taken an intercontinental flight in Maria's cousin's suitcase, probably wrapped for safekeeping in a pair of granny panties, was so mortally revolting to me that I was forced to excuse myself immediately.

"Where you goin' now?" My grandmother was obviously vexed.

"Bathroom," I managed through gritted teeth. To mask the sound of my retching, I turned the sink and shower on full blast and flushed the toilet continuously.

"Wat's da matter wit you?" Nonny yelled, banging on the door. "Watta you doin' in my bat-room? Stop wastin' da water!"

Her meddling was as bad as Lorenzo covering my mouth mid-spew, almost more than I could stand.

Eventually, I made it to the eleven-week mark and got back the results of my prenatal screening test, which were normal. This was the point at which David and I had agreed to share the news with people and yet, I didn't feel ready. My boobs swelled so much that I had to buy new bras and my belly popped enough that I had to unbutton the top of my jeans. Still, I didn't feel up to telling my family. I made up stories to cover for my obvious fatigue. I lied about why I wasn't drinking wine at dinner. The pregnancy was becoming another secret to keep, just like my eye disease. Which was odd because this wasn't bad news, not remotely. In fact, I was elated to be expecting again: it was exactly what I wanted.

I'd saved the EPT test with its double pink lines in my panty drawer; I'd see it there every morning when I got dressed, and it'd make me smile to be reminded of what was coming soon, like a kid on Christmas Eve who'd momentarily forgotten that tomorrow would be the best day of his life. I was thrilled. I was just terrified no one else would be.

"Maybe I just won't tell my family," I joked to David on our way home from dinner at my grandmother's somewhere around week fourteen of my pregnancy. "Like, ever. I'll just suddenly have another baby and I won't even say a word about it. Just business as usual."

"You're almost thirty years old," he said. "You know that, right?"

"What are you trying to say?" I countered.

"I'm trying to say, you shouldn't care what people think. It's your life. Our life."

The next day, when my parents stopped by with Junior's cheesecake, I decided David was right. I handed a sonogram photo from our last doctor's visit to my mother.

"What is this?" she asked. "Is this—this isn't Lorenzo?"

"No," I told her. "It's his brother or sister."

Then came the look—shock and fear and excitement all balled into one overladen moment, taxing the muscles of my mother's face. It was, as I'd anticipated, uncomfortable. But immediately, I felt a thousand-ton weight lift off my shoulders.

"Is this a joke?" she asked, looking at my father. He turned to me expectantly, as if this were a very distinct possibility.

"No," I replied, a nervous laughter erupting from my throat. "Surprise! I'm pregnant! Isn't it *great*?"

Then, just like they had the first time, my parents composed themselves: my dad giving me a hug and my mother making a joke about where the hell were we going to put another child in this shoe-box rat hole of an apartment? Later that night, though, she called to voice some genuine concerns, in the process breaking the decadelong code of silence about my eye disease: Didn't the doctors tell me that pregnancy could speed up the disease? How was I going to keep up with two kids under three years of age? Had I given this any thought? Did I have a plan?

What a ridiculous question.

"Of course I have a plan," I assured my mother. In fact, I had a few plans. The first was called "At All Costs, Ignore Encroaching Blindness." The second was, "Panic." The third, a bit more detailed, was "Make Grand Commitments to Do Impossible Things," and it included action items such as:

- Try not to give babies incurable disease
- Never lose children in public—Use neon colors? Leashes? GPS?

- Explain vision loss to kids so they don't feel ashamed of their own limitations
- Teach kids ASAP to identify colors, read, and cross streets safely

Then came the big item, the one thing I knew had the potential to make everything work out okay yet was, for some reason, nearly impossible:

- Tell people about visual impairment! You CANNOT do this ALONE! STOP BEING SO GODDAMNED PROUD AND STUBBORN!

That was as far as I'd gotten. After that I'd have to wing it.

One part of the plan I figured I could tackle now was telling Lorenzo about my eyes. He was only two but I felt confident he could grasp it. After all, the kid was already reciting Shakespeare. The day he farted in the bathtub and remarked, "Bubble, bubble, toil and trouble," I decided he was old enough to have The Talk.

All the parenting books I'd read recommended that when broaching big, complicated subjects with young children, it was best to keep things simple and try not to inundate them with too much information. So, one afternoon while I was helping him clean up his Thomas the Tank Engine trains, I mentioned casually, "You know another reason we have to clean up? Mommy doesn't see so well and sometimes, I can't see your trains when they're on the floor. And if I don't see them I'll trip over them and get hurt and maybe even break the trains."

"No!" he cried, shocked and chagrined. "No, Mommy! My Tata!"

"Well, Mommy doesn't want to break Thomas," I clarified. "But I don't have good, strong eyes like you, so sometimes I can't see Thomas. Especially when it's dark. Mommy can't see in the dark."

"Dar? Dar? Dar?" he inquired, turning to look at me. His blue eyes were always flung open so wide, ever inquisitive, always watching. When he blinked, I felt like he was swallowing the pictures. His was a look so unguarded, it made me feel like I should stand sentry, to make certain nothing harmful slipped in.

I tried to remind myself that what I was revealing wasn't harmful; in fact, it was just the opposite.

"Yes, in the dark, at nighttime, Mommy's eyes don't work as well as other people's," I replied, then paused. That seemed like enough information for now, a good two-year-old-sized morsel. "So will you help Mommy? Will you clean up your trains?"

"'Kay," he agreed, picking up Percy and handing it to me. Then he ran behind the couch to hide while he took a dump in his diaper. And just like that, the conversation was over. Now he knew. One less person I'd have to lie to.

Between throwing up, drafting plans, and breaking uncomfortable news to family members, being pregnant with Baby Number Two was onerous. I didn't pipe Mozart into my womb and take four thousand photos of my swelling belly, like I had with Lorenzo. The weeks flew by in a haze of exhaustion. When the time came for my five-month sonogram, I arrived half an hour late to the appointment, couldn't find my insurance card, and was on the phone, shouting instructions to Nonny about how to get Lorenzo to nap, when the technician came into the exam room.

"You ready?" she asked David and me.

"Yep," I assured her, putting my phone away.

Out of the blackness on the monitor emerged a profile, hazy and grainy but familiar enough for me to distinguish—a baby's face with eyes and nose and chin. All of a sudden I was reminded that there was an actual human being growing inside of me; it was so surprising that I laughed out loud. The technician pointed out the baby's two arms, two legs, two kidneys and though these were impossible for me to make out, I felt enormous relief at having her identify them in the right location and quantity.

Then, she turned a knob on the machine and a bass sound filled the room. When I first heard Lorenzo's fetal heartbeat, I was terrified. It sounded impossibly, unreasonably fast and I was convinced that he'd developed early hyperactivity from the few extra cups of coffee I sipped on the sly. This time, my baby's heart just sounded strong and sure, like a metronome.

"Heart sounds good," the technician said. "Now let's take a look." Within a few seconds she was nodding and pointing to the screen where I could see a flickering, an alternation of light and dark in the center of the baby's chest. It moved in synchronicity with the sound.

There are two hearts beating in me, I thought.

Then the technician sucked her teeth and smiled. "How cute! She has the hiccups."

I scrutinized the screen for a second before registering what she'd said.

"She?" I repeated.

The technician nodded and magnified a section of the baby's body that I surmised were the private parts. There was no way I could make them out, not only because the screen was too murky but because I was sobbing convulsively, a choking cry that made my belly shake and the image fuzz. The technician said she'd give us a minute and handed me a box of tissues before she left.

David squeezed my hand and smiled. He knew I wasn't sad. In fact, in that one expansive moment, I felt as if I'd never been sad or scared or hurt before.

I'd managed for months to build a powerful dam of worry that kept everything else at bay, but when I heard that I had a daughter, the dam was obliterated and the big, great feelings flooded in. The kind described in prayers and religious texts. Beatitude.

"We're so lucky," I choked out to David.

Right in the center of me was a tiny person who would one day have a tiny person right in the center of her. A set of Russian nesting dolls. I couldn't see much on the screen but what I could perceive was life, an infinite promise of life. Nothing else mattered. Compared with this, everything else was just so small.

Tip #14: On taking a stroll

City sidewalks are crowded, and not just with people.

Near the curb, you'll find signposts, lampposts, hydrants, meters, trees, bike racks, and those plastic dispensers housing free newspapers that no one ever takes.

Near the buildings, you'll find benches, planters, kiddie rides, sandwich boards, and cellar doors, both closed and open.

To regular people, these are unremarkable elements of the sidewalk landscape. To you, they are obstacles, and you have two options for dealing with them.

Provided you have a small child, you can use your stroller as a buffer, so that the front wheels encounter the obstacle before you and your baby do. To execute this safely, you'll need a sturdy SUV-type stroller with a big jogging wheel that juts out way in front; use an umbrella stroller and your child will serve as the buffer, which is the opposite of what you want. If this sounds a lot like using a stroller as a mobility cane, that's because it *is* that, exactly.

Of course, you could just take a middle-of-the-road approach. Literally. Stick to the center of the sidewalk. You'll still crash into people, of course, but people are softer than fire hydrants.

14. DR. RIGHT

"Are you comfortable?" came a woman's voice from somewhere in the dark.

I had to laugh. Was she kidding?

The voice laughed, too: "I mean, considering?"

"I'm as comfortable as a person can be with electrodes on their eyeballs," I assured her. "Besides, now that I've been through childbirth twice, the ERG doesn't seem so bad anymore."

The memory of those contractions was still fresh in my mind from eight months before, when my daughter, Rosa, was born. Mine hadn't been one of those lightning-fast second deliveries I'd heard tell of; in fact, labor had taken almost as long as the first time around, though it was infinitely more pleasant since I wasn't breaking my water during Thanksgiving dinner. Plus, this time, I was intimately familiar with the gift I'd soon be getting, a life-changing treasure— the epidural. And the baby too, of course.

Rosa was, in fact, a dream baby. She was mellow and easygoing and looked so cherubic you'd think she'd floated right off the ceiling of the Sistine Chapel. I'd been worried that being the second-born, she'd get the equivalent of love leftovers, but that turned out to be a groundless fear. Just as I had with Lorenzo, I'd fallen hard for Rosa. Which made it difficult to leave her with my parents for a day and a night to see Dr. Goodstine and his team of research assistants in Philadelphia.

Then again, I reminded myself, *I'm doing this for her, and for Lorenzo.*

If anyone could hook me up with a clinical trial or some shot at treatment, it was Dr. Goodstine. The man was a superstar, one of the leading retinal specialists in the world. And, almost as important, he and his team were just about the nicest damn people I'd ever had the pleasure of meeting. Linda, who was in charge of conducting the electroretinagram, was so solicitous and thoughtful I felt like I was getting a five-star, luxury lab experience. A far cry from the *Clockwork Orange* episode at Dr. Hall's office.

The basic mechanics of the test remained unchanged—still the same electrode contact lenses with the same freaky wires attached—but Linda's little touches made the process humane. She brought me lattes and snacks from the vending machine. She let David come in to hold my hand.

And the music. First, it was Dinah Washington's velvety vibrato filling the pitch-dark room, and now John Lennon was singing to Yoko about calling out her name in the middle of a shave. It was a small gift that felt enormous. The music gave me something to focus on when I felt the urge to blink and it kept me calm, which was not easy after nine continuous hours of tests.

"Am I almost done?" I asked Linda.

"I think after this, there's just one more test Dr. Goodstine wants to do," she assured me.

"Okay," I agreed, "but am I almost done with this one?"

"Not quite yet," she replied and I knew this meant we'd only just begun. I'd learned over the past nine hours that Linda was an expert spin-doctor, always accentuating the positive. She didn't lie, she just didn't offer details that might cause a patient to panic. When I'd arrived at 8:00 A.M. and asked how long the tests would take, she'd answered, "Dr. Goodstine is very thorough. We'll be sure to feed you lunch." Had she told me that I'd still be there at dinnertime, I probably would have walked right out the door, no matter how lucky I was to have gotten the appointment.

I'd waited nearly a year to be seen by Dr. Goodstine and now I understood why: he saw exactly one patient a week. The patients were also research subjects and as such, we agreed to a host of tests that might not have much impact for us personally but would shed light on the disease as a whole. My pupils had been dilated, my blood drawn, my DNA analyzed, and the parameters of my visual field plumbed more thoroughly than Marco Polo exploring China. Not that I was complaining. I did, however, have needs.

"Linda?" I called. "I'm sorry. I just—I need to pump."

She didn't say anything for a second, so I clarified: "My breasts."

"Ahhhhh, right, yes," she replied. "We'll take a break."

Within a few minutes, I was detached from one machine and plugged into another. The assistants made themselves scarce but David was ushered in, to keep me company. We used a flashlight to set up the pump, so my eyes could stay acclimated to the dark.

We sat in silence for a second, listening to the rhythmic *whoosh* of the pump interspersed with the *plink* of milk drops hitting the bottom of the bottle.

"I feel like a guinea pig crossed with a cow," I observed, holding a flange in each hand.

"Yes, but on the upside, we won't have to stop to get the baby a souvenir."

"And she's worth it," I said. "I fucking love that girl."

Rosa was, indeed, almost too good to be true. Not only was she bright and beautiful and smiley, she was reasonable, which is a character trait not commonly found in infants. She ate her peas. She traveled well, cooing in the double stroller as I plowed down pedestrians who dared to tread on my turf—the center of the sidewalk. Most importantly, she slept. When we'd tried to sleep-train Lorenzo by letting him cry it out at four months old, he'd screamed for a full hour the first night, and the second, and the third, and between his screaming and my grandmother's ("Chile abuse! Dis is CHILE ABUSE!"), we lost our resolve and went back to rocking him to sleep. Consequently, at nearly three years old, the kid could only doze off with a team of trained professionals soothing him. When we sleep-trained Rosa, she cried for five minutes before drifting off to the land of nod. We'd hit the baby jackpot.

In fact, we'd hit the jackpot in general. Though I'd spent my pregnancy panicking about how I was going to handle two kids who were two years apart with shrinking vision and an incurable aversion to being honest about my situation, ever since I'd had the baby, I'd felt relieved. Things were going more smoothly than I'd expected, even for the newly minted big brother.

It was true that he'd ask on a daily basis, "When is that baby going back in your belly?" and he did get apoplectic when I nursed her—"NO! DO NOT MILK THAT BABY!"—but for the most part, he went about his business as though she didn't exist, which was, as far as I was concerned, the safest situation for everyone. Since Lorenzo was home with me, we had plenty of quality time during the baby's naps, which were frequent and generous. Even as a toddler, Lorenzo was shaping up to be as big a bookworm as I'd been, and he'd clamber onto my lap and listen to page after page of Maurice Sendak or Mo Willems or sometimes even big-kid books like *Charlotte's Web*. With the baby sleeping soundly and my sweet boy sharing one of my passions with me, I felt like I'd reached parenting nirvana. Icing on the cake was the fact that I could still make out the print of the chapter books. I mean, I needed to be in a well-lit room and I needed to be holding the book in such a way that the natural light hit the page just right, but still, I was getting by without much hitch in my giddy-up.

And now I'd found Dr. Goodstine, my dream doctor. Tall and unassuming with a pointy gray beard and glasses, Dr. Goodstine's eyes were gentle. He had an unmistakably paternal air about him. The man had even given me eye patches to bring home for Lorenzo, so he could play pirate. He got it. Finally, a doctor who understood that I was a person, not just a collection of cells. Back when I was nineteen, I didn't think that was such a tall order but after having seen a slew of specialists, Dr. Don't-Shoot-the-Messenger Hall and Dr. Don't-Tell-Me-Your-Feelings Turner included, I knew just how rare it was.

It had taken years for me to find Dr. Goodstine, but he was worth the wait. When the last test was completed at almost 7:00 P.M., he invited David and me into his office to talk. After devoting eleven hours to my case, he spent another hour just talking to us, explaining everything in real-person language, answering every one of our questions, even ones that would've had Dr. Turner calling in the men in white suits, such as "Do you know other women with RP who have kids? Are their kids okay? I mean, they didn't accidentally walk them out into traffic or anything, right? What I'm doing is not totally insane—is it?"

I'm sure he thought I could benefit from a brief sojourn in a mental health facility, but he answered my questions, probably because he guessed I didn't have anyone else who could.

Dr. Goodstine had good news, too. Well, good news and bad news. On the bright side, even though it seemed to me that my pregnancies had sped up my vision loss, there was no compelling evidence of that in the test results. Yes, I'd lost a few degrees of my visual field, but nothing drastic. My visual acuity was considerably worse, but this was probably because—and here was the bad news— I'd developed cataracts. It was a common development in RP patients and nothing to worry about, he assured me. In fact, the cataracts could possibly be removed if they got significant enough, although I'd have to judge first whether the improvement in my vision was worth the surgery. Decoded, what that meant was: I might be so blind by then, there'd be no point.

And, of course, he mentioned, I did have some edemas in my eyes—well, not edemas exactly, just swelling that was edema-like—but they probably weren't worth treating with medication since the gain was minimal and the side effects were somewhat bothersome.

I smiled, thinking of Dr. Turner's failed experiment. Here was a test I'd given Dr. Goodstine, and he'd passed with flying colors.

When we were finally through, he recommended a killer place for Philly cheese steaks on our way out of town, and walked us to the elevators.

I thanked him profusely, pumping his hand with both my hands. How could I communicate how much his competence and kindness meant to me? The man had devoted his life to finding a cure for my strange, rare disease. He spent every day, all day in that lab, working on it. Knowing that made me feel enormously hopeful. Dr. Goodstine was on the case. It didn't matter if he found a cure in time for me, or even if he ever found a cure at all. He was *trying*. How could I explain what that meant? I couldn't, of course, but I gave it a shot.

"God bless you," I blurted out, and then there was no shutting me up. "That sounds crazy I know. I mean, I sound like my grandmother, but really, God bless you, Dr. Goodstine. You're a good, good man and I'll never forget you."

He grinned. "Well, I'll be seeing you again. Call me in two or three years, and we'll bring you in to see how things are going. And maybe, by then, I'll have something more promising in the way of treatment."

On the ride back to New York, I called my parents, who'd just put the kids to bed, and relayed Dr. Goodstine's rosy report.

"See?" my mother said. "Everything is going to be all right."

It did appear that way.

And then Rosa started walking.

Tip #15: On keeping track of toddlers

The best option would be to confine your toddler to a crib, day and night, until such a time as they develop impulse control. Sadly, that's frowned upon.

Particularly in public, you'll want to make the most of audible clues. Avoid cultivating strong, silent types; in this respect only, loud motor-mouths are exactly what you want. Belled collars will get you a visit from Child Protective Services but belled anklets will look bohemian and cool in a vaguely Southeast Asian way. Squeaky sneakers, aka "squeakers," are also socially accepted, though hearing that irritating sound every time your child takes a step may afford you mental problems to go along with your visual ones.

15. GOOD MOMMY

Damnit, I thought, *not again.*

It was a sunny spring afternoon and I was sitting on a bench in the playground near my house holding a naked, filthy babydoll named Bobby. I had my daughter's doll but not my daughter.

Where the hell is she? I thought, turning my head toward the slide where I saw two-year-old Rosa a minute ago playing with her big brother. There was Lorenzo, right where I'd left him, pretending to be sucked headfirst into a lava pit. Rosa, however, was not with him.

She was not thundering across the shaky bridge or shimmying down the fireman pole. She was not in the sandbox or attempting to reach the monkey bars. She was not in this playground, as far as I could tell.

I mobilized for action by rising to my feet, making sure to keep a hold of Bobby's beanbag body; I wouldn't lose the beloved doll, too. My heart picked up speed until it was racing so fast all I could hear was the sound of my blood pumping in my ears.

Why did I take my eyes off her? I fumed. *I should have learned my lesson by now.*

I'd just looked away for a minute to locate the sippy cup that had fallen out of my diaper bag, but still, I cursed myself for not knowing better. Then I cursed myself for wasting time cursing myself. I needed to take action. I had taken my toddler to a crowded public playground in the heart of New York City and I had lost her. As I pissed away precious minutes standing there, she could be darting out of the playground gate—damn those laissez-faire parents who never shut the gate behind them—and running toward the four-lane intersection just steps away. She could be wandering into the bodega on the corner, or striking up a conversation with the unsettling middle-aged man who sat near the tire swing but never had any children with him. I could not just stand there.

Do something, I told myself. *Now. Go. Move.*

"Lorenzo," I called, walking fast over to the slide. "Your sister. Where's your sister?"

He shrugged before hurtling himself down the slide, bellowing his head off as he simulated being burned alive by hot magma. He was not, after all, his sister's keeper.

This is exactly why I need to tell people about my eyesight, I thought, *so I don't rely on a four-year-old to help me parent.*

Now I was running, darting around monkey bars, peering up the spiral slide. My fist was squeezed tight around Bobby's soft hand, her body jerking this way and that as I rushed one way, then changed directions, second-guessing myself.

Come on, honey, I thought. *Come find Mommy.*

I tried to strategize but my brain had stopped working, filled instead with two words screaming in repetition: *my baby my baby my baby.*

I needed to assess if it was time to get help—another mom, the police, someone who would do what I couldn't and find my daughter—but I couldn't assess anything because my brain had short-circuited. I couldn't even judge how long it'd been that I'd been looking: one minute? five? ten? What was she wearing? I didn't remember. Where had I seen her last? I'd already forgotten. Did I have a recent picture?

No, damnit, no, went the wail inside my head, *this cannot be happening.*

I reached the playground gate, which was ajar, and then there was nowhere else to go. I was sweating. Panting. Dizzy.

I closed my eyes.

Please, I prayed, *please, just let me find her and I will never let this happen again.*

I called her name, questioningly at first, and again, in a higher pitch. I called it three, four times, sending my voice out like a fishing line to catch her.

please please please

"Mommy!"

I swiveled to the sound. There she was, sitting on the same bench where I had been sitting a few minutes before, swinging her tiny feet, clad in pink Stride Rites, and holding a snack bag of Goldfish. Her eyes, electric blue like the center of a flame, were smiling at me and she waved one chubby, crummy hand energetically in my direction.

The sudden relief upset my equilibrium so much I thought for a second I was going to hurl.

But instead, I walked over slowly, sat down beside her, and pulled her onto my lap. Maybe the weight of her against my chest would stop me from having a full-on heart attack.

I wanted to give her a stern talking-to about running away but I couldn't because chances were, she'd been sitting there the whole time.

I wanted to say something—*I'm sorry. I'm trying my best. I'll do better.*—but it would be insane to think I could explain my predicament to a two-year-old. I couldn't explain my predicament to grown-ups. That is, I wouldn't. What I did instead was scramble to keep a secret that kept getting harder and harder to hide. I protected the secret when I should be protecting my children.

I stroked Rosa's hair, for my benefit more than hers. Rosa's hair was golden, just like a fairy-tale character. Except that it wasn't just one color. There was the pale sun-bleached chunks on top but peeking out in between were darker, tawny bits, more the shade of a lion's fur. In the back it was darker still, burnt, like the crust of crème brûlée.

"Bobby was looking for you," I told her, offering her the baby-doll. She grabbed Bobby out of my still-shaking hand and smashed a handful of Goldfish against its fabric mouth. Then she smashed another handful into my mouth.

"Good mommy!" she squealed.

No, I'm not, I thought, chewing the grubby Goldfish, *I'm not a good mommy at all.*

When Rosa took her first steps, my instinct was to push her back down. I didn't do it, of course. Still, the fear that filled me was powerful and persuasive.

"You are screwed!" Fear cackled. "Good luck with that."

Immediately, Guilt popped up, sounding eerily like my mother.

"What kind of a mother lets Fear in, at a moment like this?" she chastised, clucking her teeth. "Some people should never have kids."

Then, just in the nick of time, Joy rushed in, doing back hand-springs and waving her pom poms madly, and soon I was shrieking and applauding, oohing and ahhing, and repeating incessantly "What a BIG GIRL!" which is precisely the protocol detailed in the Milestones section of the Mother of the Year Handbook.

This will be fine, I thought to myself. *I can handle this.*

I was, of course, dead wrong. I couldn't even begin to handle it.

In learning to walk, Rosa was coming into her own, blossoming into the girl she was destined to be.

That girl wasn't mellow, not even moderately.

That girl was a balls-to-the-wall, thrill-seeking, high-flying speed demon.

That girl was a firecracker with a mischievous sense of humor. And I now see that her first great prank was leading us to believe, for the better part of a year, that she was our easy child.

People have different names for the category of child my daughter fit into as a toddler. Laissez-faire folks called her "a free spirit," the practical-minded thought she was "high-maintenance," and old-school disciplinarians deemed her a "hellion." But the phrase just about everyone agreed on is "a handful." When Rosa was between the ages of one and three, you could count on someone observing, "Wow, that one is really a handful, huh?" every single time we stepped outside.

I was spared having to think of a reply because I'd be too busy grabbing her by her collar before she stepped into oncoming traffic, or yanking her back from petting a dead rat, or knocking a shard of glass out of her hand before she swallowed it.

Don't get me wrong. From the start, I loved my daughter's exuberance. I was awestruck and inspired by her spirit. Which is why it was really too bad that I had to spend every waking second trying to crush it.

What else could I do? I wanted to keep the kid around, after all. Shielding that whirling dervish from harm would've been an uphill battle for a normal parent, much less one who was already half blind and had another young child to care for.

As soon as she walked, she ran, and as soon as she ran, I knew I had a problem. A big, fucking problem.

It's not a problem unique to visually impaired people. In fact, everyone that has more than one child but still only one set of eyes encounters the same challenge. Every parent has, at one point or another, lost track of their child in some crowded public space, whether it's a playground or a zoo or a supermarket—not in a serious way, not long enough to call the authorities or anything, but long enough to make you scared, sick-to-your-stomach, bargaining-with-God scared. It happens to everyone. It's just that it happened to me on a regular basis.

When it was Lorenzo I was looking for, it was almost always a false alarm. Whether it was the fact that he was my firstborn, or just his naturally cautious outlook, he was never far. When David cut the cord on his birth day, he left the million little invisible rubber bands that kept Lorenzo always bouncing back to me.

Rosa, though, just never had that back-to-Mommy boomerang. Before she could walk, she cleaved to me, but only because I was her ride. Once she got mobile, she was off like a bottle rocket, and I swear I could hear her hissing "See you, suckas!" as she whizzed past, shimmering golden hair flowing behind her like melted metal.

Rosa would run and not come back. Sometimes, if David was with me, we'd let her go, just as an experiment. I'd watch her recede farther and farther, willing her to stop, even to pause and look back. But I always lost the game of chicken, screaming, "STOP!" and then, "David! Get her! HURRY!"

So if Rosa vanished from my field of vision it was reasonable to assume that she was making tracks for the playground gate, and after that, who knew where?

Sometimes though, like the day I scoured the playground with Bobby in tow, Rosa vanished from my field of vision by just sitting down or taking a few steps away from me. Then she'd fall into one of my blind spots, which kept growing larger and less manageable like a run in a stocking. She'd be gone, even though she was just an arm's length away. The only way to prevent this from happening was to never, ever take my eyes off her, not even to look at my watch, not even to retrieve a dropped sippy cup.

Unfortunately, this made me what I'd learned from my local parenting listserv was called a "helicopter parent." A helicopter mom is one who hovers, like a helicopter, over her child, providing constant supervision and surveillance. The opposite is a "free-range mom," who gives her children the freedom to explore, manage themselves, and make mistakes.

My mother has a different word for the latter, describing them as "morons who should never have gone off birth control." According to my mother, you don't just hand over freedom to kids; you keep a viselike grip on their freedom until they wrest it from your cold, dead hands. And even then, you haunt them until their dying day, hovering over them from the afterlife.

When I hear fellow parents hearken back to the good old days when they were kids, how things were different then and they could walk to school alone, could play stickball in the street, could run to the corner for mom's cigarettes, I am dumbfounded. I didn't even get to take candy from strangers on Halloween. My mother not only chaperoned our trick-or-treating, she chauffeured us to it, driving us from one family friend's house to the next. And even then, she checked our candy before we ate it, because while one could be fairly certain Nonny's eighty-seven-year-old neighbor didn't put razor blades in the Twix, one could never be positive.

"Don't you trust me?" I'd protest, desperate to escape her force field.

"Of course I trust *you!*" she'd exclaim. "It's everyone else I don't trust!"

One of the biggest perks of becoming a mother is that you get to show your own mother how much better you can do the job. When I was pregnant, I thought that one of the ways I was going to do this was by affording my children the freedoms I hadn't been given. Let them learn from their own mistakes. Give them space to grow.

And I might have, too, if it hadn't been for my eyes. I might have shaped up to be one cool, confident, relaxed mom, standing on the sidelines at the playground, sipping my latte while chatting about gluten-free snacks or whatever the hell Supermoms talk about, looking up every so often to locate the kids but generally doing my own thing and letting them do theirs. Sounds dreamy. I bet my hair would have been fuller and my skin clearer and my ass tighter, too.

Instead, I ended up a greasy-haired, baggy-eyed, wilted-ass helicopter mom. Except that hovering is too gentle a word for what I did. "Pursuing" is more like it. As soon as I set those kids free, my goal was to catch them back up again, which entailed endless Keystone Cop chase scenes on the playground.

It didn't take much experimentation to figure out that if I even dabbled in free-range parenting, my kids would end up in the ER and I'd end up institutionalized—and that was best-case scenario. Case in point: the Harvest Festival Fiasco.

It was early October and our go-to Park Slope playground was hosting a Harvest Festival, filled with the old-school country-fair fare we urbanites don't get much exposure to and thus go crazy for: pony rides, a petting zoo, pumpkin painting. By the time David and I rolled in with our double stroller, containing four-year-old Lorenzo and two-year-old Rosa, the place was mobbed like a subway platform at rush hour. To make matters worse, the kids immediately headed in opposite directions.

"Owsah," demanded Rosa, her pink bejeweled binky lodged in her mouth. In the sunlight, her eyes were the color of a Tiffany's box, and like the gemstones you'd find inside, they glinted, cut with sharp edges.

"Mommy doesn't understand when you talk with the paci in your mouth," I explained for the five millionth time that day. Eventually we'd have to pull the plug on the paci but it was the only thing that made Rosa remotely sedate and I couldn't face a world without it quite yet.

Rosa pulled the paci out of her mouth and enunciated clearly, "Orsey. Orrrr-seeeey." Then she threw in for good measure, "Neigh, neigh, neigh." I always got the feeling with her that I was the child and she was the beleaguered adult trying to be patient with my limited abilities but finding it very difficult. Having clarified her demand, she popped the paci back in her mouth and resumed sucking.

"No, no, no! I don't wanna go on the horsey!" shrieked Lorenzo. "Yucky yuck yuck! I wanna make a punkin."

Unlike any kid I'd ever met, Lorenzo actively disliked animals; he found them loud, smelly, dull, and coarse—in all respects revolting.

"I'll take him to the pumpkins and you do the pony ride," David strategized. Divide and conquer was always a good plan and I knew David had opted for the pumpkins because, like Lorenzo, he had no love lost for creatures that stomped in their own feces.

I left the double stroller in the Stroller Parking Area and securely took my toddler by the hand.

"We're going to the horseys," I explained. "But you have to hold Mommy's hand. No running away. Got it?"

She nodded persuasively. And she did hold my hand, the whole ten steps to the ticket table. But as soon as she realized that we would not be immediately hopping on the pony's back and would instead have to wait on a long, serpentine line, she let go and started climbing on the wooden fence that encircled the pony corral.

"Hey there!" came a voice behind me. I turned and saw Heather, the mother of a boy in Lorenzo's preschool class. Heather had three children: one Lorenzo's age, one Rosa's age, and a baby she was currently carrying in an indigo sling. All three of her offspring looked like they'd been bred to appear in Gap ads, with gray-blue eyes and chestnut hair, and all three of them were quiet and agreeable. They were interested in the right things—the son was crazy for soccer and the daughter, ballet—and they could entertain themselves for the better part of an hour by flipping through picture books. I'd had Heather's son over for a playdate one day and had been depressed for hours afterward by how competently he'd been raised. He'd asked to wash his hands upon entering the apartment, cleaned up his blocks when he was done playing, chose milk over juice, and made sure to place his cup at what he called "twelve o'clock," directly in front of his bowlful of Goldfish. My own son had somehow spilled the lidded cup all over his front, saturating the coat of cracker crumbs that had been deposited there. When Heather, ever mindful of reciprocity, had invited us over for a playdate, she'd offered the kids kale chips and smoothies. To this day, when I see smoothies, I feel shitty and subpar.

Heather was the superest of Supermoms, and her seemingly effortless excellence at everything made me toxic with jealousy.

"I was waving at you for like five minutes," Heather laughed. "Then I thought I'd just come over."

"Oh yeah?" I said, embarrassed. "Sorry. It's such a madhouse here."

I had made it a habit of blaming crowds and glare and distraction when I didn't see people wave at me, and this time it was almost believable.

"I know, huh. How great is all this?" she gushed, gesturing at the cornucopia of activities.

"Yeah, it's *amazing*," I agreed, kicking myself for having taken a negative approach and trying now to meet her positivity or, ideally, outdo it. "Especially the pony rides. Rosa *loves* ponies."

I gestured over at Rosa who had one leg over the top of the fence.

"No no no, honey, we can't ride the horsey yet," I explained, hoping to mask my frustration with a singsong voice.

Rosa glared at me as I pried her freakishly strong fingers off the fence. It wasn't just the color of Rosa's eyes that were intense. Like hands, they gesticulated. Her lids were limber, narrowing in anger, snapping open like window shades to express surprise or fear. The rhythm of her lashes told stories—fluttering from nerves, beating out a bass to concentrate, unblinking in defiance. And her blond brows, so energetic, danced in their places like back-up singers. Her eyes were like a stage where a spectacular was always in progress. Which was captivating, to be sure, but also, exhausting.

As soon as I put Rosa back on the ground, she started climbing up the fence post again. I felt like Sisyphus.

"Where's the rest of your brood?" I asked Heather.

"Oh, they're around here somewhere," she replied breezily. "Dmitri's working today so I figured we'd spend the afternoon here."

If their dad isn't watching them, I thought, *who the hell is?* How could she be so blithe and unconcerned about their lack of supervision? And, more importantly, how uncool and uptight did I seem by comparison?

"But I should get them soon because I have to throw a dinner party tonight for Dmitri's family and I still need to find a few more place settings. There's going to be twenty of us."

The last remark almost sounded like a complaint but just before it veered into negativity, she hastened to add: "But it'll be great and give the kids a chance to practice their Greek."

She's making a homemade meal for twenty people? I marveled. *I can't get it together enough to make a bowl of pasta for two kids. And even if I could, our table wouldn't fit six people, not even very thin guests who are used to confined spaces.*

My silent spiral into self-loathing was interrupted by Heather adding, "But you must know how it is. Your kids speak Italian, right?"

"Ummm, not really," I confessed. "I tried with Lorenzo a little but my husband doesn't speak and I'm not so fluent anymore and it just got too hard."

"Yeah," she nodded sympathetically. "It *is* hard."

Not so hard she couldn't pull it off, I thought.

"Oh, looks like you're moving on up," Heather observed, gesturing at the gap in the line in front of me, which I hadn't noticed. Like people waving to me from down the block, gaps in the line were something I almost never noticed without having them pointed out.

"Okay, Rosa, let's go," I called out, turning to where my daughter had been a minute ago. But when my gaze reached the fence post,

I saw Rosa was not there. I looked down the fence to the right and down the fence to the left but she wasn't there either. I felt the sick, sinking foreboding that had become so familiar since Rosa had started walking. And at that moment, I wanted to lay hands on Heather's unwrinkled neck and strangle her, right there in front of a hundred kids waiting for a pony ride. Because, unjustified though it might be, I blamed Heather 100 percent for this particular instance of losing my daughter.

She might be able to carry on a conversation looking me in the eye while her impeccably self-regulated kids roamed around; whenever she wanted to locate them, she'd just glance around with her superhuman, X-ray vision and bingo! they'd be found. But I couldn't. I couldn't talk and parent at the same time, not in crowded public spaces at least. If I wanted to keep my kid alive and in my possession, I had to train my eyes on her and not take them off, not to nod agreeably about dinner parties, not to smile in appreciation for pony rides, not for any fucking reason. I wasn't like Heather. I never would be. And in pretending I was, I'd lost my toddler in a goddamned mob scene.

"Sorry, I gotta find Rosa," I excused myself, turning in the direction of the swing set.

"Oh, she's right there!" Heather pointed to the front of the pony ride line, where Rosa was trying—and failing—to gain early entry. A bored-looking teenager was holding her at bay.

I ran over, hearing the teenager ask in no particular direction, "Does this kid belong to anybody?" but a few steps shy of the pony ride entrance, my knees encountered an obstacle and I heard a *thump*, followed by a high-pitched wail.

I looked down. At my feet was another toddler, sitting on his bum, holding his hands in the air and screaming for his dada. Toddlers, being so low to the ground, almost always fell into the big blank area in my peripheral vision; unless I was looking directly at the ground, I wouldn't see them. Rosa was used to getting knocked on her butt by Mommy. This kid was not. Thankfully, his butt was heavily padded and he appeared more startled than hurt.

Searing with embarrassment, I lifted the boy to his feet.

"I'm really sorry," I stammered. "You okay?"

He stopped crying and looked up at me curiously, probably trying to decipher my mixed messages—one minute I was knocking him down, the next I was picking him up. What was I: friend or foe?

I patted the boy on the head awkwardly in a "good-as-new" gesture and was about to take the last few steps to retrieve my own toddler when the boy's dad swooped in to the scene, lifting him into his arms and asking me: "What the hell is the matter with you?"

I assumed it was a rhetorical question.

"I'm really sorry," I repeated. "Is he okay?"

"I don't know, I guess so," he replied. "But what the hell, man?"

"I'm sorry, I just—I didn't see him there," I stammered, flushed with embarrassment and guilt and a rising anger.

"Well," he huffed, patting his son on the back even though the boy had stopped crying. "You're in a playground for God's sake. Watch where the hell you're going."

Satisfied with his rebuke, he turned his back on me and carried the boy away in the direction of the petting zoo.

With great effort, I suppressed the impulse to yell after him, "Hey! Daddy Dipshit! You wanna know what's wrong with me? I couldn't see your kid underfoot because I'm going blind. And I'm sorry if it inconvenienced you but I have begged your forgiveness and your lousy little kid is totally fine, which is more than I can say for my own, who I can't even get to because I'm too busy getting reamed out by you, you pompous, uncharitable asshole."

But if Heather thought I was uncool before, such a tirade would probably only cement this image. So I bit my tongue—as my mother would say, "'til it bled"—and by the time I'd claimed Rosa, my rage had melted into sorrow. I was crying as I buckled the baby in the stroller, though she was too busy having a crying fit of her own to notice.

Since there was no way I was returning to the pony ride line, I bought her forgiveness at the Mr. Softie truck where I got her a chocolate cone as big as her head. She stopped crying all at once but it took me a few more minutes of sitting on the curb with my sunglasses on.

I don't get to select a parenting style, I realized. *I don't have that luxury.*

As I gradually lost vision, I gradually lost choices, too. It was always little, trivial things, none of them important except when you put them all together. I didn't get to choose whether to wear heels or flats anymore; it was hard enough handling stairs and curbs in sneakers, much less teetering on four-inch stilts. I'd stopped wearing eye shadow after the third time a friend pointed out it was a bit, um, uneven; now I was forced to go bare because it was better than wearing a clown face. If it was a rainy day I couldn't opt to take the kids to their doctor's appointment with the car; it was always the bus.

One little concession that didn't feel little at all was not being able to choose what kind of watch to wear. The Swiss Army watch my grandmother had given to me at college graduation had been getting hard for me to decipher and when I'd gone to Target to replace it, I'd found there was exactly one watch with numbers large enough for me to read and it was about the biggest eyesore in manufacturing history: an oversized round watch face studded with rhinestones, with a pink pleather band. The only choice I had was whether I'd hide it under my sleeve or wear it with pride, as if it was a fully intentional fashion choice.

I chose the latter—with the watch, at least. As far as my parenting was concerned, I was still trying frantically to keep the ugly truth of my blindness hidden under my sleeve. Little hints of it kept peeking out, though, like when I knocked the toddler down, and I knew I couldn't keep it under wraps for much longer. The trouble was, after so many years, the hiding gesture had become instinct.

Pull the sleeve down. Cover up.

PART III

Tip #16: On coming to grips with your blindness

You'll have to, you know. Not "when you're ready," because you'll never be ready, but sooner or later.

Sooner is better than later.

16. RECKONING

The Park Avenue doc had said ten years, that I might have ten years of good vision left. The year of Rosa's birth marked the tenth anniversary of my diagnosis. But the anniversary came and went, and still, miraculously, it hadn't happened.

I hadn't turned Blind. Yet.

Of course, the signs that blindness was barreling its way toward me were plenty and multiplied with each passing year. First, there was the medical evidence, the visual field tests that showed my tunnel vision getting tighter, the contact lens prescriptions that kept getting stronger until Dr. Goodstine finally told me we'd hit a limit and no matter how much he adjusted the prescription, it wouldn't make my vision any better. It had gotten tough to tell if I'd put my contacts in correctly because I could hardly perceive the difference between what the world looked like when they were in and when they were out.

There were the cataracts, edemas, and development of color blindness. Thankfully, I'd already taught Lorenzo his colors so he could keep me from looking like I was getting dressed in the dark, which I basically was. You know you're headed toward disaster when you rely on a five-year-old boy for fashion advice.

But I had bigger problems than wardrobe mishaps. By Rosa's third birthday, I couldn't read regular print anymore. It was getting harder to fill out forms at the pediatricians and preschool, and I'd taken to eating a lot of Caesar salads at restaurants because I couldn't make out the print on menus but it was a safe bet that "Caesar salad" was on there somewhere. I smashed my shins into coffee tables and my forehead into monkey bars on a regular basis. I missed stairs, handshakes, sign-up sheets. I didn't recognize acquaintances until they were practically on top of me.

And I couldn't read Dr. Seuss. That was a blow.

In the midst of a day full of wiping asses, noses, and tears, and trying not to lose my children in public, nothing warmed the cockles of my heart more than curling up with my kids on the sofa to read *Green Eggs and Ham*.

Reading to the children has always been my all-time favorite parenting activity, allowing me to combine two of my great loves: literature and lying down. Consequently, I read to the kids at every possible opportunity. I didn't cook or clean the bathroom; I didn't do arts and crafts and I didn't make cupcakes from scratch for their birthdays. This was my only shot at making it to the Mother of the Year finals.

But when Rosa was three and Lorenzo was five, my failing vision turned the reading of *Green Eggs and Ham* from a treat to a tribulation.

The first few pages were easy enough to memorize.

"I am Sam!" I'd start energetically.

"Sam I am!"

Booyah. Cake walk.

But after the first few pages, things got dicey. It's not that the words were so complex or anything, but there was a world of difference between *house* and *mouse* and *box* and *fox* and the kids were hanging on every word. They didn't know it, but what they were hearing was the sound of a woman becoming illiterate. The same woman who five years earlier had consulted the OED to write her master's thesis on Virginia Woolf was now staring dumbly at a four-letter word beginning in "b." I bet you thought the road to literacy was a one-way street. Not in all cases.

"And I would eat them on a—on a—bbbb—boooo—"

My main strategy was to stall by stretching out the beginning sound of the word until I could figure out what the second half amounted to. Consequently, my kids probably think words like "here" and "there" have four syllables each.

"And I would eat them on a bo-booo—"

I knew there were two more letters to complete the word but what were they? Looked like a U, maybe. Then an L? I felt like I was failing my high school eye exam all over again. No, couldn't be UL: "boul" was not a word, not even in Seussland. I could almost make it out, damnit, I was so close. Wait, maybe it was WL. That *was* a word! It made sense. Yes! Got it!

"And I would eat them on a bowl!"

"No, Mommy!" Lorenzo piped up. "Not on a bowl! On a BOAT!"

"That's right! Good listening!" I cheered. At least I was honing my child's prereading skills. "Okay, and I would eat them on a boat, and I would eat them with a coat."

"MOMMY!" shrieked Lorenzo, giggling madly. "Not coat! GOAT! GOAT!"

"Oh, you're too smart! Soon you'll be reading this to me!" *The sooner, the better*, I added silently.

"When do these kids learn to read, anyway?" I asked David later, "Let's move that up the priority list."

"Get a magnifier," he suggested, for the umpteenth time.

"They're so much trouble," I protested. "They make me nauseous. They're expensive."

The truth was, I'd tried the kind they sell by the register at pharmacies and bookstores and they hardly helped at all, certainly not enough to compensate for the trouble of locating them in the epic mess of my apartment and the sting of admitting that I needed one. Eventually, I'd need a serious, industrial-strength magnifier, but not yet. I wasn't that bad off yet.

The curious thing about living with a slow-burning degenerative disease is that the progression never feels gradual, even though all medical evidence proves that it is.

I know that my eyesight is eroding slowly, a few more rods and cones every day, some months faster than others, but for the most part, slow and steady. But that's not the way I experience the loss. The image I see doesn't gradually get fuzzier and fuzzier like when you adjust the focus on a manual camera: the aperture doesn't slowly close in, tighter and tighter. From my perspective, my vision holds steady, the disease seemingly paused, until suddenly it takes a giant leap forward, like Pac Man bit a huge chunk out of it. When that happens, suddenly I can't do something I could do the day before. One day, I can read the demarcations on an Infant's Motrin measuring cup and the next day, I can't. One day, I can put eyeliner on straight and the next day, I can't. I perceive the loss of my vision through the loss of things I'm able to do and that loss, though years in the making, doesn't feel gentle. Every time it happens, it is sharp, shocking, cruel, like a fast jab to the solar plexus. I am never prepared.

So just after Rosa turned three, when I received an invitation to a birthday party for one of my best friends, Vivian, I grumbled and cursed but I didn't say "No fucking way." I was nervous about going, but I thought I could manage.

One of the very best things about having children, besides the heart-exploding love, is the fact that you have a get-out-of-jail-free card for most social events for at least two years. Coworker's retirement dinner? Regrets, baby's got a cold. Neighbor's Superbowl party? Regrets, baby's napping. Family reunion? Regrets, baby's teething something awful. That excuse is worth the pain of childbirth, particularly a birth with an epidural.

The excuse was especially valuable to me because most of these social functions occur after dark. Being night-blind, I sometimes forget that not everyone thinks nighttime sucks raw sewage. It always comes as a surprise to me that many of my friends, particularly the single ones, actively enjoy the night, so much so that they create a whole life within its bounds. This is what people call a "nightlife." I have found that people who have a nightlife aren't content with just having theirs, they want *you* to have one too, and they won't stop inviting you to dinners and cocktail parties until you've got a nightlife of your very own.

Thanks to having my kids two years apart, I got almost five years of maternity leave from my nightlife and I enjoyed every minute of it spent in my pajamas on the couch. But when Rosa turned three, my get-out-of-jail-free card expired. I had kids now, not babies, and there was no good reason I couldn't leave them with their daddy.

Except that I needed their daddy to come along with me. I never said as much to David when I asked him to be my plus-one at a party but we both knew that it wasn't only his charming company I wanted. After years of practice, David had learned exactly how to help me navigate in the dark, and even more importantly, he'd learned to do it so surreptitiously that no one would notice. A few close friends, including Viv, knew about my vision problems, but we'd hardly ever discussed it since the diagnosis, and I hadn't mentioned that in the past twelve years, things had, ummm, deteriorated a bit. There were no two ways about it: David was the safety pin holding my shoddy nightlife together.

David hadn't enjoyed his position as my seeing-eye guy when we were living in LA and he didn't enjoy it now, either. The hermit in him loathed being an escort and having to make small talk, and the Honest Abe in him hated the cover-up. More than once, he pointed out that as long as I refused to come out of the disability closet, he was forced to be my beard. And wasn't this part of why we moved back to New York, he asked, to give me my independence back? So, though it made my life easier to have him on my arm, whenever possible, I tried to go it alone.

Which is what I decided to do for Viv's thirty-third birthday, despite the fact that none of the event details boded well for my success. None of our mutual friends were able to attend. The party started at 9:00 P.M., way after the forgiving window of dusk. And the venue was a new hotspot in the West Village. Not only was it totally unfamiliar to me, but I knew it'd be dim, because if there is one thing you can count on, it's that the hipper the bar, the darker it is.

I seriously considered telling Vivian that we were out of town or Rosa had the croup again but I'd done that for the past three years and Viv was one of my best friends. I was beginning to feel like an asshole, in addition to a liar.

Besides, I thought, what the hell happened to carpe diem? What the hell happened to living like there's no tomorrow? After a day of potty training and volunteering at kindergarten recess, I deserved a night of empty talk and overpriced cocktails.

Screw it, I decided. *You only live once.*

That evening, I unearthed the blow drier, dusted off the dangly earrings, and spent a good twenty minutes applying makeup in the magnifying mirror. With the help of cutting-edge breast-support technology courtesy of Victoria's Secret, I was able to turn back the clock to my prebreastfeeding splendor. I put on heels, figuring I might break an ankle but I wouldn't be holding a baby, so even if I did, it'd be okay. When I stepped on the B train to Manhattan, I felt like my hips made an audible "va-va-voom" sound when they swayed. I was back in the game.

I didn't stumble or bump into anyone on the subway ride over. I managed to make out the street signs and locate the bar without too much trouble and I was only a half hour late, which by my clock is pretty much on time. But as I strutted toward the bar's front door, I felt my optimism falter. The place wasn't just dim, but a kind of deep, unforgiving dark I associate with Hades, or the countryside. There didn't even appear to be tea candles on the tables, which was totally unprecedented. At the very least, I could always count on a few measly tea candles.

Unbelievable, just unbelievable, I fumed, getting defensive so I didn't have to feel sad. *Isn't there some kind of legislation mandating a certain amount of illumination in a commercial establishment? I mean, this is a lawsuit just waiting to happen.*

Just like that, in the space of five seconds, I lost my mojo. Turn your back on her for a minute and she darts away, that capricious mutt. Without my mojo, without my vision, and without any transparency about my situation, how was I supposed to enter this hellhole of hipness?

It was time to strategize. Maybe Vivian would be standing by the door, waiting to receive guests—that was a possibility. Worth a shot, at least. I gave my mojo one last, pleading call, but it was too late; she was long gone. I'd have to go in without her.

Once inside the heavy glass door, it was darker than I'd even anticipated. Whatever scarce streetlight might have seeped in through the glass of the storefront was blocked by the throngs of people leaning against the windows. Vivian was not standing by the door, which I deduced because I couldn't hear her voice exclaiming, "There you are! Get your ass over here!"

I thought maybe I'd head to the bar, order a drink, and wait for Viv to pass by, but I couldn't make out where the bar was. Then the door opened behind me, and a fresh group of hipsters, in full possession of *their* mojos it seemed, lurched in and pushed me deeper into the throng.

Panic percolated inside me. There was no way to stay put; people would keep walking in, pushing me forward little by little and soon I'd be lost inside the tiny bar, unable to find the door again. I'd be stranded there, without Viv, without a drink. This wasn't just conjecture; it had happened plenty of times in the past, and I'd had to pretend I was shit-faced to explain why I couldn't find the door that was right next to me. Covering up for my disease by pretending to be a drunk was bad enough when I was a twentysomething in Hollywood; now that I was a mother of two, it was damn near disgraceful.

At the same time, I'd spent an hour getting ready and an hour on the train. I'd gotten Vivian a gift, my rack looked great, and I was so close—probably just a few feet away. It seemed insane to just turn around and go home.

I speed-dialed Viv's cell phone, which went directly to voice mail. I didn't leave a message. What would I say?

"Hi, Viv. I'm just calling because—well, you probably don't remember but twelve years ago I mentioned in passing that I was going blind and I know I've never talked about it since but now, actually, I really am pretty blind, so I can't find you in this godforsaken inferno. Please come find me before I will myself to stop breathing. It's imminent. Hurry."

I dialed her number again, hoping I'd at least hear a phone ring nearby and home in on the sound. No dice. And, to make matters worse, as I slipped the phone back in my pocket, my elbow hit the elbow of the woman next to me, who happened to be holding a full drink, which splashed all over her. Instantly, she exclaimed what I've discovered almost all people will say, when I've knocked their drink all over their dry-clean-only attire: "What the fuck?"

"Oh God, I'm sorry!" I wanted to offer a napkin or something but I couldn't locate her face, much less the napkins.

As she muttered, "shit, shit, shit" I counter-muttered, "sorry, sorry, sorry." My nervous system is set up in such a way that if I utter the word "sorry" more than three times in a ten-second interval, it activates my "abort mission" reflex and I instinctively begin to back away. In this case, backing away prompted a wave of drink-splashing, so that all around me other hipsters were muttering expletives, causing me to continue my incessant offer of apology to the bar at large.

When my back hit cold glass, I breathed a sigh of relief. It was over. I slipped out the door, and ran over to the street corner where a taxi was just pulling through the intersection. My getaway car. I jumped in and managed to tell the driver my address before I started bawling. I kept right on sobbing as I walked through the door to my apartment where David had only just put the kids to sleep.

"What are you doing back here?" he asked. I could see he was disappointed not to have the night to himself to watch zombie movies.

I blubbered out the story while he sat there getting sad, then angry. Maybe it's all men, or maybe it's just mine, but I find David's sadness is always followed by anger, which is followed by a super-mobilized plan to attack the problem. I'm sure it has to do with rage at feeling powerless but whatever the reason, it has historically been a problem for us because when I'm truly sad, epically sad, I don't want to solve anything; I just want him to watch me cry and feel really, really, really sorry for me.

"Next time, just tell Vivian that you can't see in the dark and she'll wait by the door."

"I can't," I explained. "It's humiliating."

"Of course you can," he pressed. "You're making your situation worse."

"You don't understand."

He sighed: "I know."

"I tried so hard," I sobbed.

David was quiet. I knew I was breaking his heart, but the need to unload my sadness onto someone else was too great. Someone had to know what was going on and he'd ensured that person would be him the day he signed on for better or worse.

"I tried so hard to stop it from happening but I can't anymore," I said in a rush. "I've been defeated. I am defeated."

I didn't just feel beaten in the figurative sense, but in the physical sense, too, like Fate had been dragging me around for the past twelve years by my hair and had now decided to really lay into me.

David could see that I needed some quality time alone with my self-pity so he went into the bedroom while I melted into a piping hot mess. I moaned, I wailed, I doubled over. I raised my fist to the heavens and I tried tearing at my hair like a character from Shakespeare but that actually hurts a lot.

I'd been refusing to go gently into my good night since the Park Avenue doc had told me not to shoot the messenger, but it wasn't until just then that I raged against the dying of the light. Dylan Thomas would have been proud. Anyone else would have called a mental health professional.

It wasn't about the party. The party was just the proverbial straw.

My blindness had come. Despite praying and protesting and pretending, it had come. And though the idea of it had scared me at nineteen years old, back then all I had to lose was what I didn't have yet. At thirty-two, I had everything to lose. I had been given two children who brought joy and meaning into my life with two radiant futures before them, futures I wanted to see, damnit.

I wanted to take my daughter shopping for a prom dress and keep her from buying something too short or too low-cut and I wanted to check out the shady character who was her date and shoot him a cold, crazy look that said, "If you hurt my baby, I'll slice your 'nads off." I wanted to see if my son's eyes would change from that bright cerulean shade and if he'd get acne or an Adam's apple. I wanted to check his math homework. I wanted to watch the kids from the bleachers when they played basketball or chess or did synchronized fucking swimming and I wanted to be able to cheer embarrassing things like, "That's how you get 'er done, son!" at the right moments. I wanted to straighten my son's bow tie while he waited at the altar and I wanted to see my daughter when she became a mother herself, and tell her that the baby looked just like her.

I'm not going to see those things. And it's not fair. And there's nothing I can do to change it.

So I sat on the couch and choked on my bitter pill for a long time, just like little Helen Keller throwing a colossal fit. I wept until my face ached and my eyes were swollen and there was no rancor left. Then, at long last, I cried uncle.

There was nothing I could do about the dying of the light but there was something I could do about the shame and self-flagellation and anxiety I felt every day over the secret I was keeping. I had to go blind but I didn't have to lie about it.

I was raising two children but still acting like a child myself, vain and obstinate. What kind of an example was I setting for them? Did I want them to hide essential parts of themselves that were less than perfect or even just different, because of what other people might think? I imagined Rosa and Lorenzo, all grown up, crying on their couches, ashamed of who they were, and it was like a bucket of cold water thrown in my face. I could not pass this legacy down. It would be worse than passing on my disease. It would be the wrong regret.

The time to grab life by the balls was over; it was time, instead, for me to grow a pair. I needed to redirect the strength and resourcefulness I'd devoted to covering up my disease to learning how to cope with it. I needed to learn how to keep track of my kids at the playground. I needed to learn how to go to parties in bars, how to check homework, how to shop for a prom dress—without my eyes. I needed help. And the aggravating thing about help is, you usually don't get it unless you ask.

So I sat down at the computer and wrote Vivian an email saying I'd come to the party but I couldn't find her because it was dark and my eyes aren't good in the dark anymore. David helped me edit out all the maudlin, pathetic stuff so that it was short and to the point. It was important that I get it right, not so much for the message itself, but because it signaled a shift in my policy. Within a half hour, she'd written back, saying she hadn't forgotten the news I'd shared with her twelve years ago, had often wanted to ask about it but was nervous about broaching the subject because it had seemed like I didn't want to talk about it. She was sorry I'd had to go home; next time, she said, she'd wait for me outside the bar.

The next week I made an appointment with a low-vision ophthalmologist who worked with the New York State Commission for the Blind.

"I think I'm legally blind," I said to the receptionist, "and I need to know where to go from here."

Tip #17: On cleaning house

The wonderful thing about going blind is that along with the beautiful sights, you miss unattractive ones, too. You won't see your crow's-feet or the thinning of your husband's hair. You will walk blithely by a trio of rats feasting on dogshit. And you will not notice the state of extreme filth into which your home has sunk.

Unfortunately, everyone else will.

So how do you clean what you can't see? If the filth becomes significant enough, you'll feel it, hear it, or worse, smell it. As a rule, surfaces in homes are not meant to feel sticky or oozing, not meant to make crunchy sounds when encountered or emit odors that cause you to gag. If this happens, you know it's time to clean. Attack the revolting areas with a sponge until all offensive smells, sounds, and textures are eradicated.

Alternatively, you could invite your obsessive clean freak of a mother over, hand her a bucket and bleach, and let nature take its course.

17. SKELETON IN THE CLOSET

I knew I'd have to grapple with the cane, right from the get-go. The low-vision specialist confirmed that I was, legally, blind, and as such would qualify for services with the New York State Commission for the Blind. I'd have to agree to being trained on the cane, of course. And I'd have to stop driving.

"That's no problem," I assured him. "I'm not homicidal. I haven't driven in years."

"Great," he'd replied. "And yes to the cane too, right?"

I uncrossed and recrossed my legs, shifting in the vinyl examination chair.

"Yes to the cane," I confirmed.

I didn't mean it, not even at the time. I just figured I'd deal with that problem when it arose. It was probably a moot point; as soon as I showed up at the Cane Training Correctional Facility or wherever the hell that awful business took place, the people in charge would see immediately that I didn't need a cane.

"This is *obviously* a mistake," the Cane Master would apologize. I pictured a chubby middle-aged gentleman with Coke-bottle glasses and sweat stains under his armpits.

"You don't need a cane; you're not blind like *that*." He'd smile, waving me away. "Go right on home. We'll take care of this mis-understanding."

As it turned out, both the Cane Master and the Cane Training were nothing like what I'd expected.

The first time Esperanza called, David hung up on her. He thought she was a telemarketer, raising money for a blindness charity, the kind that always sent us envelopes with fake coins glued in the address window, or depressing text printed on the envelope, things like, "Just $1 from you will help four-year-old Lukey see his first sunset!"

"No thanks, we don't want to donate," David had asserted.

A minute later the phone rang again. This time, I picked up.

"This is Esperanza Espinoza and I am not asking for donations," she'd informed me, quiet but firm. "I am your vocational therapist and mobility instructor."

I liked her immediately. The more I got to know her, the more I found to like. It was divine intervention, I think, that the Commission sent me my ideal-match Blind Guru; had they sent over the chubby gentleman of my imagination, I think I'd still be dodging his calls.

Esperanza was young and pretty, a small woman with a heart-shaped face and animated eyes. She had a consummately gentle way about her, never raised her voice or spoke a word she didn't consider first—in all ways the very opposite of me.

Esperanza was my Annie Sullivan. She exuded warmth, from her soft Spanish accent to her wavy, black bob. She was so gentle and easygoing, in fact, that it took me a few sessions to figure out exactly what she was supposed to be teaching me.

She'd introduced herself as a vocational therapist and mobility instructor, a vague title that was more or less meaningless to me, but after a while, I came to understand that she was teaching me how to be blind without accidentally killing myself. Our first few sessions were pretty painless; she'd come over, play with three-year-old Rosa for a bit, and then pass along casual tips about how to clean your kitchen effectively (frequency makes up for lack of accuracy) and how to cook pasta without burning the house down (adhere raised dots around the stove dial to mark Low, Hi, and Simmer).

Though we were about the same age, there was something inarguably maternal about her, so I wasn't surprised to find she had two young children at home, a son and a daughter two years his junior, just like my pair. We talked a lot about mothering, everything from weaning off the paci to how to get the boys to piss in the bowl.

She was full of tips, too, about parenting while partially sighted.

"Let's talk about kids and clutter," Esperanza suggested at our third or fourth meeting. I knew what would follow was essentially a public-service announcement for the blind, the kind I'd summarily dismiss were it delivered by anyone else. Esperanza's mini-lectures were so well formulated, though, and so useful, that I could not help but heed them.

"For the visually impaired, less is really more," she advised. "Keeping your belongings to a minimum helps you find things more easily and can prevent accidents."

I thought immediately of the cookie cutter incident. Just a few months before, Rosa had unearthed my collection of seasonally festive cookie cutters—Easter eggs and snowmen and jack-o-lanterns, oh my! She'd used the metal cookie cutters to take her Play-Doh work to the next level, and when she was done, she'd abandoned them on the living room floor and moved on to a science experiment that involved emptying my sample-sized bottle of Chanel into the radiator.

As I'd run across the room to rescue the heating system, and the perfume, my bare foot encountered one of the cookie cutters—the bat-shaped one, with wings spread.

"Jesus, Mary, and JOOOOSEPH!" I howled. The pain was considerable enough that all three needed invocation. "What the hell? Mommy's foot is not a COOKIE!"

At this, the children erupted into shrieks of laughter.

"Let's see if your foot has a bat on it!" Lorenzo squealed.

The fact that it did delighted the kids and infuriated me.

"That's IT!" I pronounced, "These cutters are going RIGHT in the garbage!"

I hadn't done it, of course. But now Esperanza was telling me I should, with no compunction.

I don't know where she came up with these tricks of the blind trade, since her vision seemed perfect, but she was full of them. The whole setup was odd but not unpleasant: we'd sip Earl Grey tea at my grimy kitchen table while she relayed life-saving kernels of wisdom or quizzed me on life skills.

"How can you ensure safety when cutting fruits and vegetables?"

"You mean blind people, right?"

"Yes," Esperanza confirmed.

"How do blind people safely slice vegetables?" I repeated. "Is this a trick question?"

She smiled, but I wasn't kidding.

"Ummm, I don't know . . . buy presliced frozen vegetables?" I guessed.

"Well, that's one option." Unfailingly encouraging, Esperanza would never explicitly tell me I was wrong. "But my goal is to help you retain as much independence as possible. So if you wanted to slice the vegetables yourself—"

"I don't," I assured her. "Like, even now, when I can see, I never want to slice vegetables. I'm already looking for a reason not to do it, and I feel like blindness will serve as the perfect excuse."

"I understand, but if you change your mind . . ." Despite her gentle demeanor, Esperanza was impossible to deter. She would equip me with tools to retain my independence whether I wanted them or not. "You'll just be sure to hold the vegetables in place with your upper knuckles rather than your fingertips, and use a knife with a good grip to avoid slippage."

I envisioned the future blind me, wearing sunglasses in the kitchen, preparing a magnificent roast for a dinner party—the kind I never threw now but for some reason imagined I would once I was an even less capable chef. I pictured myself taking a cleaver carefully in hand, securing a potato with my knuckles, and slicing off all four of those knuckles with one deft motion. Normal people who sliced off their knuckles could at least find them and bring them to the hospital to have them sewed back on, but I wouldn't stand a chance of locating my severed digits, especially with only one hand to grope with. What's worse, I'd then lack the fingers necessary to clean—by touch—the bloodbath in my kitchen.

Yes, slicing and dicing while blind seemed like a big risk with little payoff. But I didn't want to insult Esperanza's advice so I kept the observation to myself.

"So, are we ready to move on to cooking meats?" she asked. "Using the low-vision kitchen timer I brought?"

Because she was so genteel, she didn't inquire about the whereabouts of that timer, which I'd stashed in a box I'd mentally labeled "Blind Shit" and shoved on the top shelf of my closet.

Esperanza brought me a dozen household items designed specifically for the partially sighted, most of which were normal things blown up to three or four times their usual size, like they'd been shot with what five-year-old Lorenzo would call a Big-a-nator Ray Gun. My tiny apartment was filled with supersized stuff, like a calculator with buttons so big it took two fingers to press them down.

It was very thoughtful of her to bring over the stuff, but there was no way I could leave it out in the open. It was humiliating, tantamount to forgetting your vibrator on the coffee table. Plus, if my grandmother or mother stumbled upon the talking thermometer, they'd probably commit a double suicide.

It was bad enough explaining who Esperanza was to my grandmother. I hadn't planned on sharing any of my training odyssey with Nonny but one day Esperanza showed up a few minutes early while Nonny was still at my place, getting Rosa's stuff together so she could take her to the playground.

"Who was dat lady?" Nonny interrogated me when she returned with Rosa a few hours later.

"Esperanza?" I asked. "She's . . . she's a kind of teacher."

It's what I had told Rosa when I introduced Esperanza: "This is a teacher who helps people with bad eyes like Mommy." But though this vague explanation satisfied Rosa, it didn't satisfy my grandmother.

"Whose teacher? Lorenzo's?" Nonny persisted.

"No," I replied, starting to wish I'd just introduced her as a mommy friend. Now it was too late to back out.

"She's a—a teacher for me," I stammered.

"What kinda teacher you need?" Nonny was getting suspicious. I knew that if I didn't clear things up right away, she'd be left to her own wild speculations and would probably be calling my mother in an hour, panicking about how I had a secret lesbian Latina lover.

"She helps people who can't see so well," I explained. "The State sent her."

I thought if I could avoid the use of the word "blind" or "disease" maybe she'd swallow my casual delivery. But Nonny is no dummy and as soon as I made reference to the State she was able to read between the lines. Her expression morphed from surprised to stricken, like she'd found out the awful memory she'd dismissed as a nightmare wasn't a dream at all. Then she reached out and touched my face, saying, "Don't worry, Nicole, God's gonna help you."

"Okay, okay." I pulled away and busied myself slicing Rosa an apple using my fingertips instead of my knuckles. As usual, I hadn't been worrying, but as soon as she told me not to, I started in a hurry.

The next day, Nonny showed up with a vial of holy water from St. Peter's. She was calling in the big guns.

"Put it on you eyes," Nonny urged, her own gray-blue eyes full of anguish.

I knew she was just trying to raise my spirits but being reminded that my only shot at healing was a Bible-sized miracle did not, in fact, cheer me. So, from then on, I made sure not to schedule Esperanza's visits on a day Nonny would be around. The poor woman didn't have a big enough reserve of holy water.

After Esperanza had outfitted my house with blind-person gear, it was time to take the teaching out of the classroom. On our first foray outside, Esperanza just tagged along as I conducted business as usual, bringing Lorenzo to school, taking Rosa on errands.

"The first thing I'd like to suggest, if I might," started Esperanza, and it was a testament to how much I liked her that her politeness didn't drive me crazy, "I think you'd benefit a lot by slowing down."

"Maybe," I replied, "it's just, you know, places to go, people to see." I didn't want to tell her that I was walking at an even brisker pace than normal because I was panicked we'd run into someone I knew. I'd already decided that I would introduce Esperanza as a college friend but who knew if she'd go along with the story? Better to get back home before my cover was compromised.

"One thing you can do to compensate for your vision loss is to scan your environment," she went on. "That's where you sweep your gaze methodically from left to right and back again, a little higher each time, so you make the most of the vision you have. It's extremely helpful but it does mean you have to slow down."

"You're right." I sighed. You had to admit, the lady knew what she was talking about. "But now I think we should head back so I can give Rosa a nap."

A few minutes later, Rosa was settled in her toddler bed, and Esperanza was getting ready to wrap our session up. Before she did, though, she wanted to show me something. She reached into the small rolling suitcase she always brought and pulled out a tight white bundle, which she then placed on the kitchen table between us.

"I brought you a cane," she explained.

I looked up at her, surprised. She knew how I felt about this.

"Listen, I really appreciate it," I told her. "But I think I'll pass. I just don't need it yet."

Gently, Esperanza explained that I didn't have a choice.

"If you don't accept mobility training, we can't move any further with your case."

"Well, what's left? I mean, I feel like I know everything there is to know about being blind, A to Z. What more could anyone possibly teach me?"

I'd called the Commission because I needed, and genuinely wanted, help. But now that the process was under way and getting a bit uncomfortable, I was feeling like maybe I didn't need help so much anymore. I had tried to impart this to Esperanza a few times but she wouldn't take "Thanks for the memories and please never call me again" for an answer.

"I'm not positive about this," Esperanza answered, "but I think that after me, you're meeting with the Adaptive Technology Center." She looked at me expectantly, waiting for my reaction. I had none, seeing as I had no idea what the Adaptive Technology Center was. Sounded pretty boring.

Esperanza could tell she needed to work on her soft sell. "It's where experts help you adapt your devices—computers, phones, things like that—so you can maximize your use of them."

Ahhh, now this was interesting. "Can they teach me how to text?" I inquired casually. This was a negotiation and I didn't want to lose any leverage by letting on how desperately I wanted what was on offer.

At some point in the past five years, while I was busy having babies and going blind, the face of telecommunication had changed. Phones were no longer devices you talked on but devices you typed on instead. This presented a problem for me because no matter how much I futzed with the settings on my phone, I couldn't figure out how to make the font of the texts big enough for me to read. My phone would *ding!* and *bing!* and I'd realize that someone was trying to tell me something but I had no earthly idea who it was or what the hell they were trying to say.

The story I used to explain my aversion for texting—that I was a luddite who preferred verbal communication—was wearing thin. I felt like someone who couldn't pay the Con Ed bill but insisted a fire in the trash can was superior to central heat. Even my mother texted and my mother couldn't figure out how to microwave popcorn. I needed to get in the texting game.

Plus, if they could teach me how to text, maybe they could teach me how to use the contact list in my phone so I didn't have to memorize everyone's phone number like a person from medieval times. Maybe I could use the calendar and the email function, too. The Adaptive Technology Center had the potential to introduce me to the twenty-first century.

"I'm sure they can teach you to text." Esperanza smiled. "In fact, I'm pretty sure that if you qualify, they can set you up with a new computer and adaptive software, too."

Those sly bastards, I thought. *They've got me by the balls.*

My laptop, ten years old, was literally held together by duct tape and spontaneously shut down at least once a day. The "n" and "g" keys stuck and the delete button no longer worked. As a writer, this was not ideal. I found myself avoiding the use of certain words just because I knew they'd be a pain in the ass to type; I'd basically rid my writing of the word "noggin" (probably a good thing) and the entire gerund tense.

I desperately needed a new computer but didn't have the money for one. And now it was being offered to me, with all the fixings. It was almost worth having a degenerative eye disease. All I had to do was get trained on the cane.

So I told Esperanza I'd do it. But when she informed me that we couldn't conduct the training in the privacy of my apartment but would have to venture outside, in public, even the promise of a new computer and learning how to text could not persuade me to agree.

"I'm sorry. You know I really want to be compliant and every-thing but that's totally freaking impossible," I burst out. "People will see me. Lorenzo's school is just a few blocks away. I could run into teachers or other parents or shit, my neighbors, friends from college who live nearby. They'd want to know why I'm holding a blind per-son cane and I'd have to make up an excuse. No—no way. It's in-sane. I'm not doing it."

Esperanza recognized a nervous breakdown when she saw one approaching so she agreed to pause the training. She left the cane with me and told me to call her in a few days, when I felt up to it.

Picking the cane up with two fingers like it was a soiled diaper, I brought it into my bedroom and tossed it into the back of my closet, next to the red patent leather heels I hadn't worn in seven years and a broken suitcase I'd never get around to fixing.

Intellectually, I knew the cane was a tool that I could use as much or as little as I liked, to my advantage, not my detriment. My intellect, though, was heavily overpowered by emotion. And emo-tionally, the cane signaled doom. Not just defeat or failure but total, irrevocable, Greek-tragedy-style doom. As soon as I unfolded that cursed thing, I'd be a blind person, and there was no turning back. As soon as I took the handle in my hand and tapped it to the ground, the rest of my vision would fade to black and I'd live in a world with-out colors or shapes or patterns or faces. I'd never read again. I'd never see Moscow. I'd forget what my kids looked like. Before you could say "adaptive technology" David would divorce me, I'd go on food stamps, lose custody of the children, and end up shooting her-oin in a cardboard box under the Brooklyn Bridge. I'd sooner pick up a loaded gun than that cane.

The trouble was, not only was it impossible for me to cope with the cane, it was impossible for me to forget about it.

As the weeks went on, it became harder and harder to ignore, like a dead body I'd hidden that was getting ripe. Yes, just like a skeleton, the cane haunted me from my closet. No sooner had I shut the door on it than I began a slow, relentless emotional collapse, like a character in an Edgar Allen Poe story.

Though I'd refused to admit my blindness for twelve long years, suddenly I could think of nothing else. I went through my day painfully aware of what I was seeing and imagined what life would be like when I couldn't see it anymore. How would I tell the shampoo from the conditioner? How would I cut my steak or shave my legs or read Lorenzo's report cards or ride the subway?

But worse than speculating about the abilities I'd lose in the coming years was obsessing over what I'd lost already. This was a new phenomenon for me because ever since the summer following my diagnosis, I'd been living in a more-or-less comfortable haze of denial. The genius thing about denial—and it's really magical—is that you never have to feel bad. I couldn't feel bereft at losing little chunks of my vision if I just ignored that those pieces of the picture had been lost. I mean, I couldn't help but notice things like not being able to read the nutritional facts on cereal boxes anymore, but I immediately pushed that realization, and all the nasty, dark feelings that went along with it, down, down, down. I knew all that toxic emotional sludge was still there, inside me somewhere, but it was deep enough that I couldn't see it.

And now Esperanza had come along and dredged all that crap up, right out into the open. She forced me to look at my blindness without turning away. And, wow, did it suck. It super-sucked. It sucked big, hairy elephant balls.

Because here's the problem with stockpiling a decade's worth of grieving and trying to get it all done in a month: you end up with some highly concentrated misery.

I felt like the world was populated with the tombstones of things I used to see and couldn't anymore—the difference between pink and orange, the Canadian geese David pointed out overhead, a splinter in my daughter's foot. These losses made me feel sad, and worse, incompetent.

I realized the thousand risks I took every day that other people didn't take, all the ways I might unwittingly put my children in harm's way. For a long time, I'd walked the tightrope of vision loss without looking down and now that I had, I was terrified. I teetered with vertigo at the top of the stairs. My heart stopped whenever I led my kids off the curb to cross a street. And I had nightmares—lurid ones, more terrifying than the horror flicks David watched after I fell asleep. In the worst of them, I was undergoing a surgery in which my eyeballs were being removed. I watched myself on the operating table as a doctor plucked one eye at a time out of its socket. The worst part was the sound it made coming out—a sickening, sucking pop. I woke to a flop sweat.

"I should have never started this ordeal," I confided in David.

"It's darkest before dawn," he assured me. "Pun intended."

I stalled and rescheduled my cane training for almost two months. Then, one March morning, Lorenzo stumbled across my cane while he was searching for his bike helmet in my closet.

"What's this?" he wanted to know, holding out the compact white bundle.

I snatched the cane out of his hands, flushed and nervous.

"That's grown-up stuff," I reprimanded him. "And you're not supposed to be looking through my stuff without permission."

As I shoved the cane onto a higher shelf, out of Lorenzo's reach, my heart raced.

I am failing them, I thought. *This is not the kind of mother I want to be.*

Later that day, I called Esperanza and told her I was ready to take a walk.

Which is how I ended up standing next to the Gowanus Canal, incognito, holding a mobility cane and having a tachycardic episode.

"So, should we get started?" Esperanza asked brightly.

I tried to keep my hand from shaking. It felt like the cane was in control of me, not the other way around. I half expected it to yank me forward, right off my feet, like an overexcited Great Dane. Who knew where it would take me? Nowhere good, I expected. This time tomorrow, I'd probably be selling pencils out of a paper cup on the D train. But, I reasoned, it was better to get to my destination, no matter how miserable, than to keep on waiting to arrive, wondering like my kids did, "Are we there yet?" Better to rip the fucking Band-Aid off already.

I regarded the long white stick in my hand, whose most distinguishing characteristic was its plastic roller tip, roughly the size and shape of marshmallow. Not a terribly cutting-edge piece of equipment.

"You'd think after two millennia, someone would come up with something a little more advanced than a stick to help blind people get around," I observed. "I mean, we put men on the moon and made money paperless and developed robots that vacuum your carpet and still, I get the same tool as Helen Keller did? This is the best we can do?"

Esperanza laughed. "I can see you feel better already."

I did. I'd taken my first step without taking a step. Just like that, I'd ripped the Band-Aid off, and already, the sting was fading.

Tip #18: On glass doors

Walk into a glass door once, shame on the door. Walk into it twice, shame on you. Walk into it three times, get yourself a fucking game plan.

There are many mistakes you can brush under the rug but bashing your nose into a glass door at Starbucks and spilling scalding coffee all over your front is not one of them. Getting defensive and muttering sotto voce—"Goddamned places keep the glass so clean, I'll sue their ass," or "Would it kill you to FROST THIS SHIT?"—will only make you look like a grumpy old lady at best, mentally ill at worst.

No, here you will need to call upon your self-deprecating sense of humor, the Secretly Blind's ace in the hole. After recoiling from the glass like a circus clown, you must acknowledge that you are a moron, something to the effect of, "So I guess I do not have super powers after all," and hope the joke distracts onlookers from speculating about the cause of your extreme stupidity.

As you walk away, searing with humiliation, remember this: it's not your fault. Glass is a material engineered to be invisible. There's some witchcraft in that.

18. FELLOW FEELING

It was one of those times I wished I could disappear.

Genius move, sitting in the front row instead of by the door, I admonished myself as I sipped a urine-sample-sized cup of coffee.

Of course, I had been operating under the assumption that support groups make you feel better, not terminally hopeless.

I was sitting in the common room of an old folk's home off Grand Army Plaza, surrounded by a dozen visually impaired New Yorkers, ranging on the spectrum of unfortunate from kinda-blind like me, to Stevie Wonder–blind, to blind and kinda-deaf, too. At least a third of the assemblage were residents of the home, wielding walkers, and the others hovered around the fifty-year mark, many clutching white canes. There was even a guy in a fedora holding the leash of a seeing-eye dog. The whole scene was lit with an assault of fluorescent bulbs and it stank like disinfectant.

The good news, I tried to remind myself, was that I wouldn't run into anyone I knew here, which was one of the reasons I hadn't attended any of the previous meetings held at a coffee shop near my house. The bad news? Everything else.

"The worst of it is, I've always loved to read and now I can't make out the print anymore," an eightysomething woman named Ellie from Ocean Parkway was saying. "And of course, it's hard to get around at night and you know, I'm no spring chicken. I have to be careful now that I broke my hip. I can't be bumping into things."

It's not that I had anything against elderly people. It's just that I didn't want to be lumped into their category of physical well-being at the age of thirty-three.

With every passing moment, I sank into a deeper funk until I was doing deep breathing to get through however long until we took a break and I could make a run for it. Sitting there, listening to Ellie divulge every miserable detail of her visual decline, was like getting a colonoscopy; I'd been assured it was for my own good but it was no fun at all and I immediately understood why I'd put it off for so long.

Yes, this is exactly why I'd never attended a local support group meeting, even though I'd been receiving email notices about them for a while. On the one hand, the promise of enjoying fellow feeling among a group of people with similar challenges was tremendously enticing. On the other, what if those people turned out to be a pack of poor miserable bastards with all the vigor and hope sucked out of them? I wanted to attend the Hollywood rendering of a support group, with lots of pretty, young blind people who stayed upbeat and made the whole thing seem tragic in a sexy way. I wanted the fictionalized version, loosely based on a true story. *This* was not that. *This* was just the true story—not edited, not retouched, raw and emotional. I gave it two thumbs down.

I would've never gotten the gumption to attend a meeting at all had I not recently completed my training with the Commission for the Blind. Having survived that trial with my wits, and secret, intact, I felt like I could take on the world. The hardest part had been preparing myself emotionally to face the cane; once I took it in hand, the rest was cake. It only took a few short, incognito walks around the Gowanus to convince Esperanza that I had mastered Cane Basics.

"How do you know when you get to a street?" I asked Esperanza.

"Well, your cane will drop down from the curb. Usually."

"That's a pretty subtle indication," I countered. "I mean, is a two-inch change in elevation all that's going to keep me from getting crushed under a Mack truck?"

"You'll probably hear a slight increase in traffic noise, too," she offered.

"Also, far from foolproof," I argued. "I mean, do I even stand a chance? Aren't blind people just getting flattened like pancakes by the hundreds out here?"

She smiled, which is how she responded to what she thought were my rhetorical, and hysterical, questions. That Esperanza. I'd grown really fond of her quiet, unflappable optimism. She was an exceptional guide, my Virgil, leading me through the Inferno. I would miss her.

At our final visit, she gave me a long, tight hug.

"Do me a favor and join a support group," she urged. "I know you don't want to, and you might not like it at first, but it'll help. Trust me."

I did trust her. That Blind Guru of mine always seemed to know what she was talking about. She'd been right to force me to confront the cane; now that I had, I could toss the thing right back in my closet, and this time it lay there quiet and subdued, just another piece of junk I didn't need right now but would, someday. She'd been right about the Adaptive Technology Center, my pot of gold at the end of the rainbow. I'd gotten a new computer with all the keys intact whose screen could be magnified with one easy click, giving me access to each and every piece of information contained on the World Wide Web. I'd been introduced to some ingenious inventions that were available when my vision got worse—scanners that read your mail to you in a freaky robot voice ("Dear KNEE-cole, We. Have. Sum. Eeek-citing noose aboutyourhome. Mortgage."), portable digital magnifiers that could blow up print to a billion times its normal size, so big only a word or two appeared on the screen at a time. As Esperanza had promised, knowing that these tools were out there made me feel slightly less panicked and desperate about losing my vision.

Best of all, I learned to execute unimaginable feats of wonder on my cell phone, feats the rest of the world had mastered a decade earlier: emailing, checking the weather, and, yes, texting. The sense of triumph I felt when I sent my first text to a mommy friend—"Want 2 meet 4 coffee?"—was dizzying. Never again would I be forced to suffer the indignity of communicating with my vocal cords. And none of it would have happened if I hadn't summoned the courage to get help.

Which is why, when I saw that the blind and partially sighted support group meeting had been moved from the coffee shop to a private room in a nursing home, I thought, *I should do this. I can do this.*

I'd gotten gussied up for the meeting—skinny jeans with boots the color of milk chocolate and a floral wrap shirt—and before I left the house, I scrambled up a step stool to reach the new tube of lipstick I'd hidden on top of my armoire so that Rosa, infamous lipstick-eater, could not get to it.

"Ooooooh," three-year-old Rosa gasped as she saw me sweep the red across my lips, "why do you look so pretty, Mommy? Where you going?"

"I'm going to make a friend," I announced. "Wish me luck."

I was a tad concerned that the nursing home setting would bring me down but I endeavored to stay optimistic.

I'm sure it's a very nice nursing home, I persuaded myself on the walk over. *Probably very high-end, the sort of place you don't even know is a nursing home without being told, with fair-trade coffee and free wifi and very peppy, attractive, nice-smelling old people like my grandmother. There's no reason it has to be depressing.*

It didn't *have* to be depressing but it sure as hell was.

"I thought the cataract surgery would make things better but it didn't, so why'd they cut into my eyeballs for, I want to know?" Ellie continued a lament that was going strong after ten straight minutes. As far as I could tell, Ellie's vision problems didn't stem from a degenerative disease, but from being nigh on a hundred years old, and I had to suppress the impulse to shout, "Isn't it enough that you're still alive after a whole century? What, you want 20/20 vision on top of that?"

Franny, the group leader, a round-faced woman my mother's age who had macular degeneration, cleared her throat. Finally.

"Ellie, I'd love to hear more but I think we should probably move on so we get to everyone," she interjected.

The woman next to Ellie introduced herself; her name was Ruth and she suffered from Usher Syndrome, which as far as I could tell was like RP Plus. Not only were her retinas degenerating, her ears were eroding too, so that she was both part-blind and part-deaf.

Finding out that I had basically gotten the *good* incurable eye disease made me feel both terrifically thankful and depressed at the same time.

"I have cochlear implants, which help me hear," Ruth was saying, "but I'm finding it difficult to hear some of you so if you could speak up, I'd appreciate it."

"Yes, let's be sure and do that," agreed Franny.

"What?" Ruth asked.

"I said, let's all try and SPEAK UP," Franny repeated with a little more oomph.

"Yes, thank you," Ruth replied.

Emma, the woman sitting next to Ruth, didn't have an eye disease but was the daughter of a woman with very advanced Usher Syndrome. Her mother hadn't come because she never left the house anymore.

"It was gradual but now she's completely deaf and blind," Emma recounted, looking down at her cup of coffee. "She refused to face it while she still had sight and hearing left, so now she doesn't know what to do. She never learned Braille or how to sign in her hand, and now it's too late."

Good God, I thought, pressing my temples to relieve the tension headache I'd developed. *Is this the Ghost of Blindness Future come to scare me straight, show me how I'll end up if I don't change my prideful ways?*

If it was, it was not working. I was scared all right; too scared. It took incredible restraint not to bolt out the door and spend the next fifty years drowning in denial in an attempt to forget this ever happened.

"I have no way to communicate with her now," Emma went on, getting more choked up. "She just sits in her house with the curtains drawn, and I'm really worried. It's like she's given up on life."

At this, Emma broke down in tears.

Oh for fuck's sake, I thought, my own eyes welling up. I have always been highly susceptible to the contagion of crying. I get it from my grandmother; both of us have hair-trigger tear ducts.

The man on the other side of her, Mr. Fedora with the seeing-eye dog, reached over to console her. It took a few tries but eventually, his hand found its way to her shoulder. The rest of us just sat in agonizing silence, unable to think of anything to say.

But Ruth, who couldn't really see or hear Emma, didn't know why everyone had grown so quiet.

"What did she say?" Ruth asked in the general direction of Franny.

"She's—um—not talking now," Franny tried to answer discreetly. "She's crying."

"What?" repeated Ruth. "I can't hear you."

"She's *crying*," Franny replied more emphatically.

"What?" Ruth pressed. "I really need you to speak up."

"SHE IS NOT TALKING! SHE'S CRYING!" Franny shouted back, looking pained.

The whole exchange struck me as funny, riotously so. I knew it was just a juvenile defense mechanism—I've basically laughed away every moment of discomfort I've ever experienced—but knowing this did not make it any less hilarious. I felt like I was sitting on my sofa, eating popcorn and watching the scene in *Young Frankenstein* when the blind guy makes a mess with the soup.

A laugh percolated in my throat and the realization of how gauche a reaction that would be only made it harder to tamp down. It would be worse than the time I got tanked at my high school reunion and accidentally laughed during the moment of silence for the people who had died in our class. Suddenly I felt certain that I was going to laugh—not just a little titter but a deranged chortle that would possibly cause coffee to come out of my nose—and it would suck because I had enough problems without worrying that I was going straight to hell for being the shittiest person ever created. But just as I was about to bust a gut, I was distracted by the sound of a woman sighing behind me.

There hadn't been anyone sitting directly behind me when I came in a half hour ago and I was consumed with curiosity about who the latecomer could be, especially since she seemed to share my perspective that we were watching theater of the absurd.

Uncrossing my legs, I let the sunglasses on my lap fall to the floor, giving me an excuse to turn around and check her out. There, in a chair a few feet away, was a woman who looked to be in her early forties, with dark curly hair, black eyeglasses and dangly earrings. She did not appear to have a cane, or a seeing-eye dog or hearing aids. She looked entirely, 100 percent *normal*. She saw me looking at her and smiled. I smiled back.

Please have a horrible incurable disease, I thought.

It may sound unfeeling but I didn't want to get my hopes up that I'd found a blind friend only to discover it was a false alarm. That had happened the year before and it'd been a major disappointment.

I'd attended a lunch thrown by a national blindness organization to raise funds and awareness for the group's annual walkathon in Central Park. This was a highly unusual thing for me to do, but on offer was a free champagne brunch at one of my favorite restaurants, whose Belgian waffles with mascarpone whipped cream were enticement enough to get me in the door. Plus, I thought, it would be good for me. David couldn't come along because he was on kid duty so I was forced to fly solo.

After I'd stuck a name tag on and picked up my walkathon promotional materials—formatted, thoughtfully, in large print—I scanned the room for a place to sit and noticed a table nearly-but-not-quite-filled with twenty-something women, all meticulously made-up with designer purses hanging off their chair backs. Feeling like the new girl in the cafeteria, I asked if I could sit at their table. They welcomed me in and I listened to them talk about their friend who was planning a honeymoon in Tuscany and about the Miss Sixty sample sale they'd gone to last week.

They aren't defined by their blindness, I thought with relief. *They don't even look affected. This is where I belong.*

After the waffles had been cleared away and coffee was being served, I summoned the courage to ask what brought them to today's lunch.

"Oh, our coworker Lillian," the girl next to me said. "She has this eye disease that is going to make her blind, so every year we go to the walkathon to support her."

They didn't look affected because they weren't. I was such a moron.

"Why are *you* here?" the girl asked me.

I am, I reminded myself, *at a* "Cure Blindness" *fund-raising meeting.* If there was ever a situation in which I should feel comfortable revealing my blindness, this was it.

"Yeah, I have a friend like that, too," I lied.

As I was leaving, the girls introduced me to Lillian. She was well spoken with a pretty smile. She had enough vision left to look me in the eye and a good, steady job, far from a charity case. But she wore thick glasses, sensible shoes. She had taken Access-A-Ride over to the lunch. She didn't seem unaffected. The disease had marked her. And not only did this observation make me feel like a shallow, awful human being, it scared me.

I realized with some irony that I didn't belong with the cool girls and I didn't belong with the blind girl. I didn't belong anywhere, except far, far away from support groups.

But now, in the nursing home, it looked like I might find a friend after all. So I prayed that this dark-haired woman would be afflicted with an untreatable degenerative disease.

And she was, I found out a few minutes later when Franny called a break and the woman sidled up next to me as I filled my coffee from the box on the counter.

"What a terrible choice of venue, huh?" she said, adding creamer to her coffee. "Half these people don't even have an eye disease, they're just old. I'm Rachel, by the way. I have RP."

"Me too!" I all but squealed.

"Here," Rachel said, nodding down at her right hand, which was extended in my direction. "Want to shake hands? I know I can never handle handshakes without a warning."

This observation took my breath away. She knew what I was, and wasn't, seeing. She got it. After all these years, my entire adulthood, I'd found someone else who dreaded handshakes.

"I'm a therapist," she continued her introduction, "and I have three kids—fifteen, nine, and seven."

I gasped, audibly. Rachel laughed.

"I'm just—just so impressed," I stammered. Some door that had been soldered shut deep in my consciousness had just flown open. What I was thinking was, *I didn't know that was possible. I didn't know you were allowed to have three.*

What I said was, "I've always wanted to meet another mother with RP."

As I formed the words, I realized suddenly just how desperately

I'd wanted that, though I'd never admitted it to myself. So when Rachel suggested we take off and have an impromptu breakout session at a nearby coffee shop, I agreed readily.

As Rachel recounted her story, I hung on every word, from her diagnosis as a teenager to the visual decline that happened during her pregnancies to the oh-so-familiar trials and tribulations of child-rearing with shrinking vision. How she'd broken her ankle a few years ago when she didn't see a shoe one of her kids had left on the staircase. How she held her breath every time her kids took their annual vision test at the pediatrician's. How she'd finally taken the plunge and started using the cane at night a few years ago. I was stunned by how much our stories overlapped, but what I found truly, well, eye-opening were the ways they diverged.

Rachel wasn't the first in her family to have RP—her mother and a grandparent were diagnosed with the disease as well—and in part because of this and in part because she was just made of stronger emotional mettle, Rachel had never kept the disease a secret. Not from her kids, or her friends, not even from her employer. It was just something people knew about her, she said, and really, it wasn't a big deal.

In fact, Rachel seemed incredibly well adjusted, remarkably free of Sturm und Drang.

"Do you ever feel guilty?" I ventured when my coffee cup was almost empty. "About the kids?"

"What do you mean?" Rachel looked blankly at me, which was surprising as I'd anticipated that she'd understand exactly what I was talking about.

"I just feel so guilty whenever I bump into them or step on their feet or I can't drive them someplace," I elaborated. It was something I'd never told anyone, not even David. "Like they're paying the price for my problem."

"But all kids do, and every parent has a problem," Rachel replied. "And this one's not your fault."

"Right," I affirmed, looking down at my coffee.

"Why should you feel guilty?" Rachel was puzzled. "You're a good mother, I can tell just by talking with you."

"Yeah," I replied uneasily. This was enough support-grouping for one day. I pulled my jacket on.

"I mean it," Rachel persisted.

"Okay," I told her, lining up the zipper. "Thanks."

"You are a good mother," she repeated.

And then, moments away from my clean getaway, I crumbled. This time, no amount of chortling could keep the feeling at bay. The support-grouping had cracked open my shell and now my emotional matter was oozing out as I wiped away tears, right there in the crop-to-cup coffee shop filled with hipsters and freelancers and toddler-toting stay-at-home moms.

I'd spent five years soothing and nursing and teaching my children, and through it all, I had been carrying around the feeling that I was not good enough. I would never be good enough. My kids deserved better. For five years, I'd wanted more than anything—more than a windfall of money or a good night's sleep or an all-expenses-paid beach vacation—for someone to tell me I was a good mother, knowing the whole story. And now someone had, and I believed it.

"I'm glad I stuck it out at the meeting," I sniffled as we stood, readying to leave.

"Me too," Rachel smiled. "And you should give it another try later. There are a lot of interesting people who come and some really good information."

"Maybe," I nodded, walking toward the exit.

"Oh, watch out for the glass door," Rachel warned. "I walked right into it the last time I was here: how humiliating is that?"

We exchanged phone numbers and made a plan to get the families together for dinner. I walked home with a skip in my step, giddy and cheerful and amped up on too many cups of coffee. I'd gotten what I came for and more—a friend, and a roadmap.

Tip #19: On reading

Once you become literate, you read without even meaning to. It's just instinct; see text, decipher it. Except for when you can't see the text anymore—not well enough to discern letters and numbers, anyway. What to do then?

You could, of course, get a magnifier. That would be sensible and effective, but not very discreet. It's hard to be surreptitious staring through a massive magnifying lens á la Sherlock Fucking Holmes.

No, the obvious answer is: teach your children to read as soon as humanly possible and force them to be your personal print-to-speech translators.

What makes this strategy so ingenious is that it will look as if you're helping your kid and not the other way around. No one will guess that you're relying on a kindergartener to comparison shop at the supermarket or to tell you what service changes affect the 6 train. When you urge your little one to sound out the letters on a label or a sign or permission slip, it will simply look as if you're offering them the opportunity to nail down their reading skills.

In this way you can feign literacy and campaign for Mother of the Year at the same time. Multitasking at its finest.

19. SURRENDERING

When Lorenzo was an infant and my identity was still in flux, I attended a Mommy and Me yoga class. Yoga has never been my thing, despite the fact that I've always wanted it to be, and doing it while holding a screaming baby in a room that stank of feces did not make it more appealing. Consequently, it was my first and only Baby on Board yoga experience; it did, however, leave an indelible mark. At the beginning of class, while we were still unrolling our mats and unpacking infants, the instructor told us a story I will never forget. She had two young kids at home, she said, and she had just gotten over the stomach flu.

"There I was, throwing up and pooping myself at the same time," she recounted, her legs in lotus position, "and I actually felt relieved. Because I knew that now, I'd get a break. I'd been feeling really lousy for a day or two but not lousy enough to get out of making lunches and doing bedtime and stuff. But now with the vomiting and diarrhea, there was no way I could do it anymore. I just remember sitting there on the toilet with my face over the trash can and thinking, 'Thank God.'"

I finally understood this story the day I relinquished my driver's license. Figuratively, my ass was on the shitter and my head was in a barf bag but in reality, I was leaning over the counter at the DMV, sliding my license through the opening in the glass window.

I hadn't driven since Lorenzo was born but I'd hung on to my license. As it turns out, those suckers at the New York Department of Motor Vehicles let you renew your license for ten years at a time, never suspecting, I guess, that a person can lose most of their usable vision in that period. So I'd waltzed around town, flashing my fully functional license whenever proof of identification was called for, and every time I handed it over, I felt reassured. I couldn't be too far gone if I still had a driver's license. The little laminated card was a critical support beam in the scaffolding of my self-confidence and I treasured it, even with the awful photo of me at twenty-three, sporting a jet-black bob and a tank top emblazoned with Chinese dragons.

But a few weeks after my thirty-third birthday, my ten-year grace period ran out. The license expired. And I was forced to confront the fact that it was the last license I'd have.

I could hardly even drive my body around anymore. Navigating around at nighttime had always been hard but over the last year or two, navigating crowds even in the day had become tough; regrettable, given that in New York, crowds were difficult to avoid.

Not a day passed without me colliding into strangers on the sidewalk or subway platform, on line at the bank or at the playground. I'd come to resent dogs, because they ended up getting me into so much trouble. The tiny, yippie ones were too short to enter my central vision; inevitably I'd stomp on their tails or kick them inadvertently in the ribs as I took a step, which always prompted their owners to sweep the yelping furballs into their arms while shooting me very shaming looks. Even the bigger dogs presented a problem when they were attached to ten-foot-long leashes stretched diagonally across the sidewalk with what seemed a lot like total disregard for other pedestrians. If I had a dollar for every time I've gotten tangled up in a dog's leash like a dim-witted cartoon character, I'd be rich enough to ban dogs from Brooklyn.

It was bad enough assaulting people and domestic animals with my body, but worse was the damage I'd do with my stroller when I rolled it over the polished shoes of some businessman at rush hour or felled adorable toddlers with it. Summertime was the worst because everyone peeled off the protective armor of boots in favor of sandals, exposing the soft, unsuspecting flesh of their Achilles tendons. No matter how many times it happened, I couldn't grow accustomed to the look on strangers' faces when I rammed my stroller wheel into those tendons; the progression was usually shock, then confusion, then indignation. I always apologized profusely but that didn't make the gimped-up denizens of Brooklyn feel any better.

If I could do that much damage behind the wheel of an eleven-pound stroller, I shuddered to think what I could do behind the wheel of a car. There was no way I could ever drive again, not even to move the car on alternate side parking days. No, once I had kids and realized the value of human life, I established a zero tolerance policy for my own driving. So when my license finally expired, I had no choice but to hand it over to the authorities and get a non-driver ID instead. I'd informed myself about this process on the DMV web page entitled "Resources for the Older Driver." Already, off to a lousy start.

"I'm surrendering my license," I told the man behind the counter, trying to keep my voice down but still be heard through the glass.

He glanced down at my license and then slid it back over, along with a blank form.

"It just expired, so you don't have to give it up," he explained. "Just fill this out to renew."

I slid the license back to him decisively: "No thanks. I'm not renewing."

"It's not hard," he assured me. "All you have to do is pay the fee. And take the vision test."

It did sound simple, so simple that I was tempted to agree. But then I glanced over at the eye chart behind him and was reminded that I didn't have a choice; I could hardly make out the top line.

"Thanks but no," I persevered.

"You sure?" He raised his eyebrows. "Once you give it up, it's not so easy to get back again."

I swallowed hard. Going to the downtown Brooklyn DMV was misery enough without having to confront the tragic fact of your incurable disease, too. It wasn't this hard to *get* the license in the first place. Now it appeared that I would be forced to have a public unraveling, with sobbing and Kleenex getting passed and the whole nine yards, just to earn a shitty ID usually reserved for the ninety-and-older crowd.

I tried to keep my voice from cracking: "Yes, I'm sure. Not renewing. Surrendering."

"Suit yourself." The man shrugged, as if he'd learned after so many years not to attempt to talk sense to the wackadoos who passed by his window.

When I walked out of the DMV a half hour later, I'd lost the right to drive, and there was no way I'd get it back. It was gone. I felt a great sadness, like some precious possession I'd been clutching had just dropped from my palm into a sewer grating. But I felt relief, too, at the finality of it. Gone was the pressure of trying to hold on. And it occurred to me that when the day finally came that I couldn't leave the house without my cane, I might feel liberated.

Ever since my visit to the Park Avenue doctor, I've been losing my foothold in the world of the sighted, getting pulled slowly but inexorably into the liminal space between vision and blindness. I have fought the pull ferociously, by denying, by pretending, even by getting help. With increasing desperation, I scramble to stay in the world of the sighted, even just a little bit, because the worst thing, I've always thought, would be to let go completely. But that day at the DMV, it dawned on me that maybe the worst thing was being trapped in the place in between.

In fact, giving up my license felt so great after the fact that I started experimenting with giving up other things. One day David came home to find I'd packed up all our glassware for the Salvation Army and purchased plastic cups from Ikea instead.

"No more broken glasses!" I pronounced.

I relocated the dome magnifier Esperanza had given me—a thick semicircle of glass just the shape and size of a souvenir snow globe—from the back of my closet to my purse, where it would actually come in handy. It still took me a few months to work up the courage to take it out in public and the first time I did, I burned with embarrassment, certain that everyone on the uptown 2 train was staring at me. Of course, the wonderful thing about riding the New York City subway is that nobody gives a crap what weird stuff you do. Whatever freaky shit you're doing, they've seen or done freakier. Once I saw a morbidly obese women shaving her eyebrows with a disposable razor and I hardly even looked twice. I'd have to undress and stick the magnifier up my ass to get anyone to even glance in my direction. This became clear soon enough, and within a few minutes, my cheeks stopped burning and I could relax. The next time I pulled the magnifier out of my purse, I was less embarrassed and the time after that was easier still.

It reminded me of breastfeeding in public. The first time I bared my breast in a restaurant to nurse Lorenzo, I felt like I was using a public bathroom with the door open. I was sure that in the few seconds it took for me to cover up with a pashmina, I'd scandalized the whole place with my exposed nipple; I was just waiting for someone to shout, "This is a family establishment, ma'am!" After a few weeks though, I'd dispensed with the pashmina entirely. I'd unbutton my shirt nearly down to the navel and yank out my massive, leaking breast in one swift gesture, flashing my goods like I was in a *Girls Gone Wild* video. Like I tell my kids, everything gets easier with practice.

Even after I became more comfortable with my magnifier, I

tried to use it surreptitiously. This was difficult to do around children because kids, it turns out, can't keep their big yappers shut. My own kids had gotten accustomed to the magnifier but other kids would notice and get all curious. Once I was using it very discreetly to sign up for parent-teacher conferences at Rosa's nursery school and a little boy piped up.

"Hey, that's cool! What is it? Can I have a turn? Are you a wizard?"

I looked around to check for witnesses. All clear.

"Yes," I whispered, narrowing my eyes to slits, "I am."

His lip started to tremble and he ran back to his rug spot.

Of course, I tried not to use the magnifier in front of people I knew because that would entail me explaining the whole story and the thing I was most loath to do, more than receive cane training or go to support groups, was explain the whole story, especially to people I'd known for years. I knew they'd think it was odd that I'd never told them something as big and important as this. Of course, the longer I waited, the more odd it got.

My trouble was, I didn't know where to start. It was a harder conversation to have than you'd think, mainly because there was never a natural segue. I kept waiting to be in the middle of a conversation that offered a smooth transition. Like, maybe someone would one day bring up Stevie Wonder, and then I'd say, "Hey, speaking of blind people, did I ever tell you I am? Blind, that is?" Or maybe, if I waited long enough, my friends would confess a secret of their own to me, like they'd had gender reassignment surgery or had worked for the CIA or something, and then I'd say, "I'm glad you brought that up because there's something I've been meaning to tell you, too."

When neither of these opportunities presented themselves, I had no choice but to create my own lead-in. The one I used most frequently was: "Okay, so here's something crazy. . . ." Admittedly not the smoothest transition but it didn't matter much because I blurted it out so quickly my conversation partner hardly had a chance to process the words before I was moving on to: "I sort of have this secret incurable disease where I'm going blind." Then, I'd break into a manic, nervous laughter, which did not increase anyone's comfort level.

When I told one of my closest mommy friends, Grace, she was genuinely confused.

"Wait, are you kidding?" she asked.

The realization that I was bungling things miserably only made me more nervous. And when the going gets tough, I laugh harder.

"No!" I guffawed.

"'No' you don't have a secret disease or 'no' you're not kidding?" Grace looked perplexed.

"No—not kidding." I managed through my peals of laughter. "Yes—am—going—blind."

She tilted her head and looked at me quizzically.

"Also," I panted, catching my breath, "I have emotional problems. Obviously. So can we never discuss this again?"

"Of course we have to discuss this again," she replied, furrowing her brow. "But first, back up and tell me what the hell you're talking about."

After I'd shared all the pertinent details, she told me that it was actually a relief. Over the years she'd noticed strange things I did that just didn't add up, didn't jive with the kind of person she knew me to be. How I didn't shake the hand of someone she introduced me to. How I sometimes didn't see my kids, or hers, when they were standing right in front of me. Why I didn't take Lorenzo's splinter out that one time, and asked her to do it. They were just these little moments that seemed off, and it was unsettling because she knew there must be some perfectly reasonable explanation. Lo and behold, there was one. And now that she had it, all those moments made sense.

I was surprised when she thanked me for telling her, like I'd given her something she valued but of course, I had. I'd given her the truth.

Tip #20: On crossing the street

Jaywalking is one of those little luxuries you don't realize you'll miss until it's gone. Make no mistake, you will miss it, not so much the thirty seconds saved by crossing against the light, but the confidence of knowing the coast is clear after a cursory glance. The certainty of safety.

That, and not looking like a goody-goody. Because everyone jaywalks, and I mean everyone. Hunchback, arthritic old men. Groups of day care kids on an outing. Cops. But you will wait, lonely on the curb, ten seconds, twenty, thirty, looking like a bozo, because the big difference between you and these people is, they can see a car speeding their way and you cannot, not reliably at least. Your kids will want to know why, *why* they have to wait when everyone else is crossing and you will explain, as sanctimoniously as you want, that jaywalking is against the law and that you, for one, take the law seriously.

"One day you'll thank me," you'll tell them, knowing they won't, knowing they shouldn't have to. The assurance that you won't kill them accidentally is just one of those things you want your kids to take for granted.

20. MIRACLE

I've prayed for a lot of things over the years but never for a miracle. I've always felt it was better not to micromanage the divine and not to get too greedy. So when I prayed about my eyes, I mainly offered thanks for preserving my vision so far and asked for fortitude in the face of what would come.

Soon after I turned thirty-four, though, I found myself hoping, if not outright praying, for a miracle. Nothing lavish. I didn't need an old-school Let-the-Blind-Man-See cure. Just a minimiracle would suffice, or even a hint of one en route, like maybe the shrinking of my cataracts or something. It wasn't because my eyesight had gotten worse, which it had. It was because I wanted something very badly that I didn't think I could have without at least a pinky swear from someone in charge that things would hold steady for a while. I wanted another baby.

In fact, I'd wanted another baby for a long time. It wasn't a deficiency in my first and second born that made me crave another child; in fact it was just the opposite. Mothering Lorenzo and Rosa had taught me to love more intensely, more completely than I thought possible. It was like my heart had been in boot camp for six years, pumping iron and running triathlons, and had become a supersized muscle with unrivaled power. My heart craved progeny. My body craved progeny. My mind said: "Get a hold of yourself, woman."

There was no way I could indulge my desire to add another branch to the family tree. I'd been nervous about having a baby six years earlier, when Lorenzo was born, and back then I could still read Dr. Seuss. I'd been nervous about having a baby four years before, when Rosa was born, when I could still make out the labels on baby food jars.

Now, I couldn't see the sizes on clothing tags. On sunny days, the glare made it hard for me to tell when the streetlight turned from red to green. Now, I had a cane in my closet and a reduced-fare Metrocard classifying me as "disabled." I was eligible for Access-A-Ride, for crying out loud. That's how my eighty-year-old grandmother got around. She shouldn't be popping out more babies, and neither should I. It was selfish, I reasoned, to have a baby if I was incapable of safeguarding its physical well-being.

Besides, I had the family I'd always wanted, an embarrassment of riches. Asking for anything more seemed greedy and with my limited capabilities, downright irresponsible. Of course, should my capabilities become less limited for some reason, it wouldn't be irresponsible anymore. Being an optimist, I allowed for the possibility that this might happen. After all, it had happened to my mother when she was young. But in addition to being an optimist, I'm also pragmatic, so I gave my miracle a deadline. Should my stars not change by the time I was thirty-five, I decided, we should close up baby-making shop, ideally with a nice, big vasectomy. A person has to draw the line—or snip it, as the case may be—somewhere. In my mind, having to contend with "advanced maternal age" on top of all my other challenges would be too much.

Initially, I'd tossed out the miracle loophole casually, a throwaway. During the kids' early years, I didn't think much about it. It wasn't like I actually expected some shocking reversal of fortune, some deus ex machina to descend and make everything suddenly okay. But as soon as I turned thirty-four and my deadline became tangible, I found myself frantically searching for any sign of a miracle en route.

I tried to ignore the longing I felt for another child, which grew stronger and more urgent as the possibility dwindled. When I couldn't ignore the longing, I talked myself out of it.

I already have two healthy, amazing kids who I've managed not to damage yet. Why isn't that enough? How could I be so ungrateful?

I reminded myself of the relentless anxiety and guilt that had abated since Rosa became more self-sufficient. If I had another baby, I'd be right back in that emotional maelstrom again, only worse because the aperture of my vision has closed even tighter.

When I couldn't talk myself out of a third baby, I started joking about it to David. It started one evening a few weeks after we moved into the brand-new one-bedroom apartment we'd just bought, while David and I were hanging pictures up in our bedroom. It wasn't a real bedroom, but one we'd fashioned by putting up a sliding glass door that divided the large living room in half. We'd assembled an Ikea wardrobe to use as a closet and hung up blue curtains to block out the view of the electrical supply store across the street and now we were adding some finishing touches.

"The room looks great," David observed. "And it's a decent size, too."

"Yeah," I agreed. "We could even fit a bassinette next to the bed."

He looked up at me, his eyebrows raised.

"I'm joking," I assured him, putting the screws back in the toolbox.

"It doesn't sound like a joke."

"Don't be ridiculous. Of course we're not having another baby." I laughed, taking the hammer out of his hand. Then I added, "Unless you want to."

"Nicooooole," he warned, almost exactly the way Ricky Ricardo crowed "Luuuuucy . . ." when she was about to execute a hare-brained scheme.

"What?" I protested. "I'm just saying, never say never."

"Sometimes you can say 'never.' Like when you buy a one-bedroom apartment and there's already four of you living in it. Like when you say, 'We're never having any more kids.'"

"I just don't want to rule anything out without full consideration."

"Nicole," he said, looking me squarely in the eyes. "Do you want another baby?"

I made a whole bunch of faces then, unsure which one to settle on. First, "shocked-at-the-mere-suggestion," then "yeah-right-as-if!" followed by a wild, maniacal smile.

"Yeah," I confessed, "I do. A lot."

"Good God." David sighed. "You're a madwoman."

"But don't worry, I know it's crazy," I assured him. "I know we can't."

He didn't reply. He was straightening the wedding photo we'd just hung up, which showed thinner, less wrinkled versions of us locked in a synergistic kiss under the Brooklyn Bridge.

A few days later we were driving the kids to our annual apple-picking adventure, and through some great, unprecedented alignment in the stars, both children fell asleep in the backseat. I wondered silently whether this might be the miracle I was waiting for but decided that was probably stretching it.

David and I took the opportunity to seize back control of the music selection, and we chose Nina Simone. Now, Nina is breathtaking to begin with but after listening to the Backyardigans for an hour, she's a revelation. Her warming, throaty voice washed over us as she sang "Ne Me Quitte Pas" and we watched the flaming fall trees passing by our car windows. I felt relaxed enough to offer the following observation: "It's so peaceful when they're asleep. Kind of makes you want to have another one, huh?"

"Makes *who* want to?" David retorted, his left hand on the wheel and his right extracting pretzels from a bag on my lap. He was an excellent driver, so relaxed and confident, and every move seemed effortless. "Not me. Makes me want to enjoy the peace for a millisecond."

"Hardy har har." I rolled my eyes.

Then he sighed: "I thought your eyes were getting worse. Remember how hard it was for you even just a year ago when Rosa would run away?"

"Yes," I conceded, popping a minipretzel in my mouth. "It's true. It's a terrible idea. Just forget it."

Nina had gotten to the chorus.

"Unless something fantastic happens," I added.

"Are we still talking about this?" David asked.

I shrugged.

"Like what?" He was suspicious. "What fantastic thing is going to happen?"

"I don't know. We win the lottery or they make a bionic eye or I get a sign, a very clear sign that we should have a baby. Within the next year."

"Nicole," he said, shaking his head. "You're setting yourself up to be hurt."

We fell quiet and let Nina's voice seep into us, with all its heartache. When the song was over, David spoke again:

"Listen, you know I'll follow your lead on this. If you really think it's for the best, I'll do it. But you need to be sure it's for the best."

That was no small feat.

I made lists of pros and cons. The Cons list read:

Not safe for baby because of my vision
No money
No space
Pregnancy makes eyes worse?

And then, the loathsome:

What if baby gets disease?

On the Pros list there was only one item:

I want another child

I put the two lists side by side, and the conclusion was clear. No. No way. After all, I told myself, just because I want something doesn't mean I should have it. Lots of people want things they shouldn't have—extramarital sex, another drink, money from someone else's wallet. Part of being an adult is understanding that you can't always get what you want.

But then I'd have a tea party with my kids or curl up with them in the bottom bunk singing Beatles songs, and I'd think, *These kids are well cared for. And I love them, so passionately. How could it be wrong to create another life that I'd love this much? How could that be selfish?*

I'd tell myself any leap forward humankind has made was the result of an insane idea. And besides, plenty of totally blind people have babies, I'd reason. Every parent has some limitation, whether it's depression or a food addiction or a missing leg or a perpetually overdrawn bank account or an incredibly demanding job that leaves them little time to spend with their kids. This was a challenge, not a deal breaker. Getting pregnant would be a courageous move; I'd be liberating myself from making decisions based on fear.

And then I'd fall over a fire hydrant and face-plant on the sidewalk and think *What if I was holding a baby?* and it was back to the drawing board again.

How do you make an impossible decision? I don't know because I didn't. David made it for me.

On Mother's Day, at the exact halfway point between my thirty-fourth and thirty-fifth birthday, David took me out to a fancy dinner way out of our budget. I couldn't read the menu so he read it to me. After we ordered our food, he reached for my hand on the table.

"Hey, stop eating olives for a second," he said.

"But they're insanely delicious," I replied. Then I looked up. His face was fuzzy by candlelight but I could see he had a serious look in his eyes.

"What is it?" I panicked.

"No, no, it's nothing bad." He smiled. "It's just that . . . I've given it a lot of thought and I think we should have another baby."

I held my breath. This was totally unexpected.

"You want this so much and I want to give it to you," he continued. "It sounds trite but life is short. There's no time to be scared."

"Are you sure?" I stuttered. "I don't want you to feel pressured."

"I've learned how to deal with your pressure after a hundred years of marriage." He smiled. "I'm sure."

His face got fuzzier as my eyes welled up.

"But I'm not sure," I stammered.

"Yes you are." He squeezed my hand. "You're just nervous, but I'm telling you not to be. I know you'll take good care of this baby."

Not "a baby."

This baby.

Just like that, my little girl became real. Within two months, she was physically present, swimming around inside of me.

I couldn't read the instructions on the EPT test this time around but thankfully I already knew the drill. The double pink lines, I could see with no problem.

As soon as I saw them, I started to shake with relief. All of a sudden, I knew we'd made the right decision, the right one for us at least. There would be fear and anxiety and guilt and even accidents, yes. But never regret. My story line wouldn't wrap up neatly with all problems resolved, like the ending of a thirty-minute sitcom, or a Shakespeare comedy. The baby wouldn't fix everything, or anything even. But she wasn't meant to. The miracle I'd been searching for did arrive, and it wasn't a cure or a windfall or even the miracle of life. It was the ability to feel such love for a life that hadn't even come to be, knowing full well what I was up against.

I clutched the pregnancy test and admired the double pink lines. They were fierce and unapologetic, like the "Dare You" lipstick in my purse, like the tattoo on David's arm, like the self-portraits of the kids that hung on the fridge, all primary colors, all sure strokes.

EPILOGUE

Click snaps the light switch and the nursery goes dark. There's a night-light in the wall by the crib but I can't see it because my head isn't turned that way. I walk backward three careful steps to the seat of the rocking chair I know is waiting. Here, I'll nurse Lucia to sleep.

She's hungry, all right, and lunges toward my chest, panting and grunting like a chimpanzee. Now that she's six months old, she needs no guidance; she could find the breast were it hidden under a suit of armor.

"All right, honey," I tell her. "Just a second."

I feel the edge of the rocker meet the back of my knees and I surrender to its cushions. My back is aching from carrying the baby and my feet are throbbing after dragging my big kids around town— school and the playground and swimming and dinner at Nonny's.

Within ten seconds, the baby's found what she's looking for and her lips make smacking sounds. I can hear David's muffled voice reading bedtime stories to Rosa and Lorenzo in their room. "And Ida, mad, knew goblins had been there." *Outside Over There*. Must be Rosa's turn.

The baby stops nursing for a second and I feel her head turn against my arm. She must be looking at me. I swivel my face in her direction.

"Are you looking at Mommy?" I ask, "Ooooh, I'm gonna get you."

I don't need to see to find the place she likes to be kissed, right below her ear, a supple spot beside her throat. I nuzzle her there, and she laughs, a sound like popcorn crackling or little fireworks going off. *Pop poppity popop pop.* There is no better sound anywhere. My mind re-creates the picture to go with the sound, the picture I saw only five minutes ago, before I turned off the light—the crinkle-nosed grin that leaves her pink mouth agape, the eyes shining like lanterns.

The baby's eyes haven't found their color yet. When she was born, they were that newborn shade, no color really, just dark, like they'd become all pupil from being in the womb so long. Like the Eye of Horace from ancient Egyptian art—omniscient. They didn't even make tears when she cried.

Now they are regular, of-this-earth eyes. They fix on points of interest, track me as I move around the room. Except that they hardly ever blink. It's like she's so hungry to see things, she gulps it all in without stopping to chew. And preternatural, too, is how the color keeps changing; some weeks cobalt, then lighter, like a robin's egg, then a darker cerulean again. Always blue, though, like her daddy. All my babies have eyes like their daddy; I just hope they stay that way.

Poppity pop pop goes her laugh. She gives herself over so fully to the joy of it, and so do I, warm and full with the sound.

When she's finished laughing, I switch her over to nurse on the other side where she tugs away with renewed vigor.

I lay my head back on the blanket that covers the chair, a pink and green striped number that Nonny knit for me when I was a teenager. Nonny is the baby's best friend. When she sees her great-grandmother, Lucia's face lights up and she pumps her little arms up and down like she's about to achieve lift-off. I can hear them singing Italian lullabies together as soon as I get off the elevator to pick Lucia up from my grandmother's apartment; there's Nonny's vibrato on top and Lucia's just as loud underneath, only without words. Thinking of this puts me in a melodic mood so I start singing Nonny's favorite *ninna-nanna*, the same one she sang to me, the same one I sang to Rosa and Lorenzo.

E stato il vento che ha fatta cadere la cana . . .

Lorenzo always laughs when he hears me sing this, ever since I translated the words for him. He was delighted to discover the lyrics weren't about stars a-twinkling and cradles a-rocking, as he'd assumed. He likes to sing along but in English: "I walked down the streeeeet and came to a restauraaaaant. Give me half a carafe of wiiiiiine. Daddy wants to goooo toooo sleeeeep."

As soon as she hears my voice, the baby stops nursing and croons along.

"Ahhhhhhhh," she intones, like a Gregorian monk. "Ahhhhhh-hhhhh."

Her chanting is interrupted by a yawn. She finds her way back to the breast and nurses again, her rhythm slowing. With one hand, she reaches up toward my throat to grab hold of the necklace she knows is there.

When Rosa was born, David gave me the necklace: a silver chain with two thin disc-shaped pendants hanging off. One disc read "Rosa" and the other "Lorenzo" and on the backs were the kids' birthdates. When Lucia was born, I added a disc to the mix. Now when I walk, the pendants jangle like bells and the tintinnabulation reminds me of what a full family we are.

David, instead, wears tattoos. On one pec "Lorenzo," on the other "Rosa," and for Lucia's first birthday, he'll get her name on his left deltoid, opposite the place where my name is. Then he'll be balanced, a quartet of names making things symmetrical. The tattoos are beautiful and I've thought about getting a set of my own. But I don't need them; my body is already marked by my children. The faded stretch marks on my abdomen. The teardrop shape of my breasts. The creases on my forehead and the crow's-feet. I don't know the marks you'd find in the cellular material of my eyes, but it doesn't matter. Whatever the loss, it was nothing compared to what I've gained.

When Lucia was born, I couldn't stop crying. I was overcome by hormones and nerves to be sure, but also by gratitude. I just kept breaking down and thanking David. It was different from when I had Lorenzo and Rosa, not because I was happier or more grateful but because I knew how close we'd come to missing this. When I thought of how we almost chose No, almost chose to play it safe, my heart ached with relief. How lucky I was. The word *treasure* doesn't encompass it.

I feel the same thing now, rocking Lucia in the dark. There is nothing missing from the moment. The fact that I can't see her takes nothing away. Maybe it's because in the morning, I will see her again. But maybe it's because even without my eyes, there is enough. I stroke the curve of her cranium. I breathe in her slightly sour milk smell. I listen to the soft moaning sounds that signal she's almost asleep. This isn't just enough. It's an unimaginable abundance.

From the other room, I hear a lull in proceedings and then David's voice again reading *The Lion, the Witch and the Wardrobe.* It's Lorenzo's turn to choose a story. In the chapter I read to the kids last night; Aslan was killed. Tonight, I think, he will be resurrected.

Lucia lets go of my necklace and pulls her tiny fist back. *Thump.* She pats my sternum.

It's what she does when she's about to drift off to sleep, a soothing technique like rubbing feet together or twirling hair around a finger. She's probably mirroring the way I pat her after she nurses, to bring up bubbles. But I can't imagine my patting soothes her as much as hers does me. She pats my chest again, her own inimitable rhythm.

Thump   *Thump*   *Thump*

Her pudgy fist lands a little below my collarbone, on the right side. Just where my heart is beating, slow and steady, full to bursting with wonder.

Thump   *Thump*

ACKNOWLEDGMENTS

It takes a village to raise a child and nothing less to make a book. Without the tireless support of the following people, and many others too numerous to name, this book would not have been possible. Profound thanks.

To my agent and stalwart advocate, Michael Bourret: thank you for believing in me even when all I had to offer was a picture book about a disfigured alley cat. To my editor, Sara Goodman, for impeccable guidance and faith. Your vision breathed life into this book; thanks for taking a leap of faith.

To all the big brains at St. Martin's for their incredible efforts in support of the book: Lisa Senz, Kelsey Lawrence, and everyone in sales and marketing, the wonderful Katie Bassel, glamorous Angie Glammarino, and Susannah Noel.

To Ryan Knighton and Jim Knipfel, whose haunting, hysterical memoirs on blindness were revelations, personally and professionally: thanks for letting me join the RP Boy's Club. To the illustrious Domenica Ruta, Alice Bradley, Rachel DeWoskin, and Jenny Bowman, for reading the book and offering such kind words of support.

To Debra Nussbaum Cohen, for allowing me to imagine the impossible. My youngest child thanks you, too, for that.

To the members of the FFB group, Park Slope chapter, whose

generosity of spirit, ingenuity, and courage are an inspiration. Thank you for welcoming me into your fold. You can't cure my RP, but you may yet treat my whopping case of Denial.

To all my doctors, but especially to Dr. Jacobson and his team of Mensa card-carrying geniuses, who are in the business of making miracles. Thank you, not just for your indefatigable research but for the gift of hope.

To Grace Quinones, sent to my doorstep with her bag of tricks by a higher power. I am profoundly grateful for your kindness, your warmth, and your saintly patience.

To those illimitably generous souls who serve not just as my readers but as my cheerleaders and my dear, dear friends: Miranda Beverly-Whittemore, Claire Lundberg, Emily Raboteau, and the woman who restores my sanity daily, Kimberly McCreight. A million thanks to all of you for suffering through draft upon draft, for answering dumb and incessant questions, for brainstorming, problem solving, and never once saying, "Enough already!" even when it clearly was. Without your sage counsel, my book would be a steaming pile of dung, and without your friendship, I couldn't make it through the day.

To Michelle Flax, Merrie Koehlert, and Amelia Shaw, for endless encouragement and compassion.

To the world's greatest in-laws, Dan and Susie Greengold, for their love and unwavering support in every possible way. A special shout-out to Meg Greengold, who rescued the title of this book.

To the fierce and beautiful Cavaricci women—Franca, Alanna, and Sidney—for undying loyalty and faith (and countless hours of babysitting).

To Melissa Harty, my first partner in greatness, who has had my back ever since she sang backup in my Madonna cover band at the age of six. To Courtney Caccavo, for seeing greatness in me. I will aspire to fill the mammoth shoes of the Nicole-saurus you imagined me to be.

I could write a whole other book describing the debt owed to my parents, my indomitable, selfless, loyal parents, Dr. Nicholas and Margaret Caccavo. Thank you for loving me intensely, completely, without bounds or qualifications. Thank you for being there, always—when I needed you, when I didn't, and when I insisted I didn't but really did anyway. Thank you for making the right decisions even when they weren't easy, for working tirelessly so I didn't have to, for telling me over and over again that I could be anything I wanted to be. Everything I am is because of you.

To my children. Since the moment each of you was born, you have been the cures, the miracles, the reasons why. I'm terrifically proud of this book, but you are my greatest creations, and ever will be. I thank you for bringing a light into my life that can never be extinguished, for blessing my days with boundless joy, laughter, and meaning. More than anything, though, I thank God for giving you to me, my bella, my nina, and my beamish boy, three gifts beyond all imagining, gifts I will work my life to deserve.

To my best friend, my partner in all things, the root of the root and the bud of the bud, my husband, David. There is no force greater than my love for you, except perhaps my debt to you, which defies measure and description. You gave me the seed of this book and the water and sunlight I used to make it grow. Thank you for your keen eye, your discerning ear, your strength, your generosity, your patience, your great, selfless sacrifices. Thank you for our family. Thank you for a love that makes everything always possible. 'Til the wheels come off, and after that, too.

And to my grandmother, Verusca Zangoli Cavaricci, who made me me. You have taught me by example how to be a mother, a daughter, and a sister, a storyteller and a friend, a person of faith and goodness. *Mille graze per tutti i doni che mi hai dato: le canzoni, i racconti, le cene, per le lacrime e i sorrisi, e per il tuo grande amore. Ti voglio tanto, ma tanto bene, per sempre.*